# Promoting Prosperity

# Promoting Prosperity

## *Via Economic and Technology Policy*

Stuart S. Nagel

LEXINGTON BOOKS
*Lanham • Boulder • New York • Oxford*

*HD*
*75*
*.N34*
*2000*

*Dedicated to Bill Gates*
*for the work he did in ushering in the computer technology revolution.*
*Also dedicated to Bill Clinton*
*for the work he did in ushering in the longest period*
*of economic prosperity in U.S. history.*

LEXINGTON BOOKS

Published in the United States of America
by Lexington Books
4720 Boston Way, Lanham, Maryland 20706

12 Hid's Copse Road
Cumnor Hill, Oxford OX2 9JJ, England

British Library Cataloguing in Publication Information Available

**Library of Congress Cataloging-in-Publication Data**

Nagel, Stuart S., 1934–
    Promoting prosperity : via economic and technology policy / Stuart S. Nagel.
        p. cm.
    Includes index.
    ISBN 0-7391-0163-3 (cloth : alk. paper)
        1. Economic development. 2. Factors of production. 3. Technology and state. 4.
    Economic Policy.

HD 75 .N34 2000
338.9'26—dc21

                                                                            00-034795

Printed in the United States of America

⊖™ The paper used in this publication meets the minimum requirements of American
National Standard for Information Sciences—Permanence of Paper for Printed Library
Materials, ANSI/NISO Z39.48–1992.

# Contents

**Part Three  Technology Policy**

# Tables

# Acknowledgments

In this book, the word "we" is frequently used rather than "I," reflecting the fact that this book was written in collaboration with the associate editors of the Everett Dirksen-Adlai Stevenson Institute of International Policy Studies, the Miriam K. Mills Research Center for Super-Optimizing Analysis and Developing Nations, and the Policy Studies Organization.

Those people especially include Julian Nam, Diem-My Bui, Yuki Llewellyn, Sara Eckart, and Carol Burger who worked on the camera-ready copy. Those people also include the collaborative drafting people, Deni Hoffman, Connie Schradt, Julie Glassman, Paula Erwin, and Carolyn Tryon.

Other highly helpful people include Matthew Beth and Jane Young, and especially Joyce Nagel, who is the administrator and business manager for all three of the previously mentioned organizations.

# Introduction

This is the prosperity volume in a three-volume set on peace, prosperity, and democracy. Each volume, however, is self-sufficient, although there may be reciprocal causation among peace, prosperity, and democracy.

All three volumes approach peace, prosperity, and democracy from both a domestic and an international perspective. The domestic perspective may appear to emphasize the United States, but it is generally applicable to almost any country because of the broad nature of the issues.

In *Promoting Prosperity*, the domestic material deals with both economic policy and technology policy. This is because prosperity, or economic growth, depends heavily on the introduction of new technologies and the training of the labor force to deal with the new technologies, as well as other economic and technological factors.

The economic part is divided in two sections. The first section deals with improving the total economy and covers: (1) employment and inflation, (2) spending, taxing, and the deficit, and (3) organizing the economy. The second section deals with improving the factors of production and covers: (1) land and agriculture, (2) labor and management, and (3) capital, business, and consumers.

The technology part is also divided into two sections. The first section deals with improving urban and regional planning. It covers: (1) environmental protection, (2) housing, and (3) transportation. The second section deals with better policy toward physical and biological science. It covers: (1) energy, (2) health care, and (3) technological innovation.

In the international section, all three volumes emphasize the role of multiple nations in promoting peace, prosperity, or democracy. The multiple nations could take the form of a world organization, such as the United Nations or the World Heath Organization. The multiplicity might occur by way of a regional organization such as the European Union (which is mainly economic), the North Atlantic Treaty Organization (which is mainly peace-promoting), or the Helsinki Watch (which is mainly focused on democracy), along with counterparts from other world regions. Sometimes the multiplicity may consist of just a couple of neighboring countries trying successfully, or unsuccessfully, to promote peace, prosperity, or democracy, such as the current neighbors of the Congo.

As applied to prosperity policy we are especially talking about:

1.  The exchange of goods.
2.  The international exchange of goods including issues that relate to national competitiveness, tariffs, exporting, importing, and tariff agreements.
3.  The international exchange of people including immigration policy, international refugees, and volunteerism in technical assistance.
4.  The international exchange of factories including foreign factories coming to the United States and U.S. factories going abroad.
5.  General international exchange facilitators including monetary exchange rates and international economic communities.

## Win-Win Analysis

This book contains many win-win or super-optimizing tables. A typical win-win table shows the goals to be achieved on the columns, the alternatives for achieving them on the rows, and relations between the alternatives and the goals in the cells. There are generally two sets of goals consisting of conservative goals and liberal goals. There are generally two sets of alternatives consisting of conservative alternatives and liberal alternatives

Conservative goals tend to emphasize what is good for business, national security, and dominant ethnic groups whereas liberal goals tend to emphasize what is good for labor, consumers, the environment, civil liberties, and minority ethnic groups. Conservative alternatives tend to emphasize relying on the marketplace. Liberal alternatives tend to emphasize relying on government regulation.

There is generally little controversy over what the conservative and liberal goals and liberal alternatives are. There is much controversy over which goals are more important and which alternatives should be adopted. Solutions that are win-win are those that are capable of achieving the conservative goals even more than the conservative alternatives and simultaneously capable of achieving the liberal goals even more than the liberal alternatives. The object of the tables and the analysis is to suggest one or more win-win solutions for each policy controversy.

The phrase "win-win solution" is used throughout this book to refer to solutions or proposals that exceed the best expecta-tions of liberals, conservatives, and other major groups in a controversy. The wording comes from the idea that both sides win beyond their best expectations, not just beyond their worst expectations which is what happens in typical compromises. Sometimes the phrase "super-optimum solution" (SOS) is used to suggest that the proposal or - solution surpasses the optimum of liberals and conservatives. Win-win is shorter and more catchy than super-optimum but has the disadvantage of being frequently used to refer to any positive outcome even if it does not exceed the best expectations of the major viewpoints, parties, sides, litigants, or disputants.

One can determine the conservative and liberal goals and alternatives for each policy controversy by reading newspapers like the *New York Times*, news magazines like *Time*, and textbooks that deal with public policy controversies. Determining a win-win solution may involve some creativity, but more important is a knowledge of other solutions that have been adopted in public policy controversies so that one can draw an analogy to the controversy under discussion.

There may be controversy over how strong the relations are between the alternatives and the goals, especially if one attempts to measure them as a percentile. There is much greater agreement if one is only interested in whether the direction of the relation is positive

(+), negative (-), or neither (0). That is sufficient for clarifying that conservative alternatives do relatively well on conservative goals more so than liberal alternatives, and that liberal alternatives do relatively well on liberal goals more so than conservatives. For an alternative to be a win-win alternative, it has to do especially well on both conservative and liberal goals.

For greater detail on the relations between alternatives and goals, one can have a five-point scale rather than a three-point scale. The numbers, words, and symbols corresponding to those five points might be:

5 or ++ means the alternative is highly conducive to the goal
4 or + means mildly conducive to the goal
3 or 0 means neither conducive or adverse to the goal
2 or - means mildly adverse to the goal
1 or -- means highly adverse

Conservatives and liberals tend to perceive that conservative alternatives receive a relations score of 4 with conservative goals, and liberal alternatives receive a relations score of 4 with liberal goals. Conservative alternatives receive a relations score of only 2 with liberal goals, and liberal alternatives receive a relations score of only 2 with conservative goals. These are default scores subject to appropriate adjustments where conservatives and liberals might be closer together or further apart, while preserving 5 or ++ for a maximum positive relation and 1 or -- for a maximum negative relation.

Likewise, there may be controversy over the quantitative importance of the goals to conservatives, liberals, and others. There is much greater agreement if one simply recognizes that conservatives by definition value conservative goals more so than liberals, and liberals value liberal goals more so than conservatives. Neutrals value both sets of goals approximately equally. Win-win solutions are capable of achieving a higher score than conservative alternatives using conservative weights and a higher score than liberal alternatives using liberal weights.

For greater detail on the relative weights or measures of importance of the goals, one can have a three-point scale. The numbers, words, and symbols corresponding to those three-points might be:

3 or +++ means highly important
2 or ++ means moderate importance
1 or + means relatively less important but still having positive value

Conservatives give a weight of 3 to conservative goals and a weight of 1 to liberal goals. Liberals give a weight of 3 to liberal goals and a weight of 1 to conservative goals. Neutrals give a moderate weight of 2 to both sets of goals. These are default scores subject to appropriate adjustments where conservatives and liberals might be closer together or further apart, while maintaining 3 for a maximum and 0 for a minimum.

In light of these definitions and the way in which win-win tables are organized, these tables should be considered as serving the purpose of clarifying the nature of each of the controversies discussed in this book–tools for pedagogical or teaching purposes rather than data based tables showing correlation coefficients, percentages, or other quantitative data.

They are based on empirical observation of the nature of the political world and political controversies, but they do not come from questionnaire surveys or from quantitative content analysis, or from other quantitative data-gathering techniques. They are not only helpful in clarifying the policy controversies, but also in showing how a proposed win-win solution relates to the goals and alternatives which are the components of the policy controversies.

It is important to note that the tables are suggestive and not conclusions. They suggest possible win-win solutions, but any win-win solution may be subject to improvement by incorporating new ideas. In that sense, win-win solutions may only be temporary answers to policy controversies or only good for a certain location under certain conditions. They are thus stimulators of ideas for answering policy questions rather than answers that are good for all times and all places.

In order for a proposal to be a full win-win solution, the proposal must not only be capable of exceeding the best expectations of conservatives, liberals, and other major viewpoints simultaneously–the proposal must also be capable of being implemented. That means it must have economic, technological, social, political, international, and legal feasibility. The text accompanying the tables in this book frequently addresses the need to overcome these feasibility hurdles. A win-win solution must also exceed the conservative, liberal, or other alternatives by a substantial enough margin so that it is not easily shot down if the relations or other aspects of the analysis are misperceived

These generic aspects of win-win analysis are discussed in other books such as Nagel, *Super-Optimum Solutions and Win-Win Policy: Basic Concepts and Principles* (Quorum Books, 1997), and Nagel, *Public Policy Evaluation: Making Super-Optimum Decisions* (Ashgate, 1998). The purpose of these three volumes on promoting peace, prosperity, and democracy is to go beyond those generic books and get into numerous specific policy disputes that relate to legal, international, economic, technology, social, and political controversies.

The combination of the cross-cutting methodology books and these more focused substance books adds up to a win-win combination for understanding and applying win-win analysis. The editors of these books from the Dirksen-Stevenson Policy Institute, the MKM Research Center, and the Policy Studies Organization look forward to seeing these books and applications improved upon in the future, across countries, to better promote peace, prosperity, and democracy.

# PART ONE

# PROSPERITY IN GENERAL

# Chapter 1

## Domestic Prosperity

### Unemployment and Inflation

#### Conservative Alternatives

Doing nothing is not likely to worsen unemployment or inflation, but it is also not likely to help. Decreasing the money supply and increasing interest rates may decrease inflation, but increase unemployment. The same is true of decreasing government spending and increasing taxes. The Reaganomics approach involves decreasing taxes to stimulate employment, and decreasing domestic spending to reduce inflation. The Democratic counterpart as of 1980 was to increase employment through government jobs and decrease inflation through price control.

Raising interest rates to decrease inflation may have the effect of decreasing prices by reducing spending from borrowed money. Those benefits may be more than offset by the undesirable effects on reducing the ability of business to borrow for expansion, inventory, and other purposes. The reduction in spending may also have an adverse effect on employment.

Raising taxes and decreasing spending to fight inflation may not be politically feasible. It would also reduce the ability of the government to give tax breaks and well-placed subsidies to increase productivity.

## Table 1.1   Inflation and Unemployment

| ALTERNATIVES | GOALS | |
|---|---|---|
| | **Conservative**<br>Lower inflation. | **Liberal**<br>Lower unemployment. |
| **Conservative**<br>Monetary policy (change interest rates). | + | – |
| **Liberal**<br>Fiscal policy (change taxing and spending). | – | + |
| **Neutral**<br>Little of both. | 0 | 0 |
| **SOS or Win-Win**<br>Economic growth policy (increase new technologies and upgrade worker skills). | ++ | ++ |

## Liberal Alternatives

Increasing the money supply and decreasing interests may stimulate employment, but increase inflation. The same is also true of increasing government spending and reducing taxes.

Lowering interest rates to decrease unemployment may have little impact because businesses are reluctant to borrow when they are reducing their operations and sales are down. Likewise, consumers are reluctant to borrow when they are already heavily in debt and fearful of a reduction in employment or hours.

Lowering taxes and increasing spending to fight unemployment may not be politically feasible when the national debt and deficit are already too high.

## A Win-Win Alternative

Increasing the adoption of new technologies and raising the skills of workers to help to reduce inflation by: (1) increasing the productivity of labor to offset increased wages, (2) increasing the quality of goods to offset increased prices, and (3) increasing the GNP and domestic income to further offset increased prices.

Increasing the adoption of new technologies and raising the skills of workers help to reduce unemployment by: (1) making the workers more employable, (2) increasing the GNP and domestic spending to stimulate the creation of more jobs, and (3) increasing the productivity and wage rates thereby offsetting a possible reduction in hours.

The conservative alternative of having interest rates up in time of inflation and down in time of unemployment does not make sense if inflation and unemployment are simultaneously problems. That would be so if both were over 3 percent. Likewise, the liberal alternative of having a budget surplus in time of inflation and a budget deficit in time of unemployment does not make sense when both inflation and unemployment are over approximately 3 percent. One can, however, stimulate new technologies and upgrade skills when inflation and unemployment are both occurring simultaneously.

# Economic Growth and Displaced Workers

## Economic Growth

### Definition and Importance

Economic growth refers to the annual rate of increase in the gross national product or the gross domestic product. The GNP refers to all income generated in the United States even if it goes to some foreigners. The GDP refers to all income generated anywhere in the world that goes to Americans.

Economic growth is highly important because it provides the increased income that generates increased spending, taxes, jobs, money for government programs, and appropriations for dealing with schools, crimes, health, transportation, communications, food, housing, defense, new technologies, upgrading skills, etc.

*Conservative and Liberal Approaches*

The conservative approach tends to emphasize taxing and spending that is helpful to investment and business. The increased investment does stimulate economic growth. Conservatives advocate increased investment through lowering taxes on the upper income brackets and lowering the capital gains tax. They also advocate spending for highways, airports, railroads, and other expenditures that will facilitate business profits.

The liberal approach tends to emphasize taxing and spending that is helpful to consumption and workers. The increased consumption does stimulate economic growth. Liberals advocate increased consumption through lowering taxes on the lower income brackets and raising exemptions for dependents and the standard deduction. They also advocate government spending for food stamps, housing vouchers, welfare, teacher salaries, health care, and other government expenditures that result in high consumption.

*A Win-Win Package*

A SOS package can promote economic growth more directly rather than through private investment and consumption, in spite of increasing investment and consumption. Such a package might include the government providing: (1) long-term, large-scale risk capital, (2) a stimulus to competition by readily granting entry

**Table 1.2   Economic Growth**

|  | GOALS | |
| --- | --- | --- |
| **ALTERNATIVES** | **Conservative** Investment. | **Liberal** Consumption. |
| **Conservative** Trickle down. | + | – |
| **Liberal** Percolate up. | – | + |
| **Neutral** Both. | 0 | 0 |
| **SOS or Win-Win** Package.  See text. | ++ | ++ |

permits into all industries and entry of foreign goods into the United States, (3) a stimulus to business and labor to adopt new technologies and upgrade worker skills, (4) funds for relocating workers displaced by tariff reduction, immigration, new technologies, or conversion from defense production, (5) reductions in foreign tariffs to open new markets, (6) immigration policy that brings in innovative, ambitious people with needed skills, (7) free speech to encourage creativity, including suggestions to improve productivity, (8) grants, patents, and purchasing to stimulate inventions but requiring licensing to stimulate diffusion and competition, (9) an educational system that is oriented toward preparation for productive jobs and careers, and (10) conservation of natural resources and a productive, healthful environment.

Other important economic indicators besides economic growth include unemployment, inflation, and measures of income equality. Big economic growth is offset if those other indicators worsen or do not improve.

### Displaced Workers and Firms

Displacement of labor can be brought on by: (1) productivity downsizing, (2) free trade, (3) immigration, (4) civilian conversion, (5) jobs for public aid recipients, and the disabled, the elderly, minorities, and women.

The issue here is how to find jobs for displaced workers. The conservative emphasis is to leave it up to the recipient to find a job on his own and not make it a responsibility of other people.

The liberal emphasis is on the welfare agency or another government agency doing most of the job finding work. The neutral position might involve delegating the activity to a non-profit organization.

A key conservative goal is to save tax money. That means encouraging job finding to reduce welfare payments, but not incurring high fees for job finding. A key liberal goal is to find jobs for displaced workers or welfare recipients, not just to save welfare payments, but also because jobs can increase the income, quality of life, and dignity of welfare recipients. Doing so also has effects that

**Table 1.3    Equity versus Efficiency in Displacement of Labor**

| | GOALS | |
|---|---|---|
| **ALTERNATIVES** | **Conservative** Efficiency (merit or survival of the fittest). | **Liberal** Equity (i.e., fairness to those unemployed to no fault). |
| **Conservative** Marketplace. | + | – |
| **Liberal** Welfare handouts with few conditions. | – | + |
| **Neutral** Welfare with conditions: 1. No able bodied eligibles, especially males. 2. Bare minimum benefits. 3. Residence requirements. 4. Provide no due process. | 0 | 0 |
| **SOS or Win-Win** 1. Training. 2. Wage subsidy. 3. Employment agency commissions. 4. Rising GNP. 5. Relocation. 6. Welfare conditional on training and job cooperation. | ++ | ++ |

relate to multipliers, compounding, role models, and reducing illegal activities.

A SOS alternative is to contract out to a private profit-making firm at a commission of $X per welfare recipient who receives long-term employment. Half of the commission is paid after four months on the job and the other half after eight months. The firm is responsible for providing training, day care, employment leads, advice, and dispute resolution, which the government agency might otherwise provide.

This is a good example of contracting out. The profit motive stimulates more success in finding jobs than the rate of success by a government agency or a non-profit organization. The firm also has more capability than the recipient. Tax money is saved in the long run as a result of replacing welfare with work. It may also be saved in the short run by costing less money per long-term job found than the cost with a government agency or non-profit organization.

Related activities can also help displaced business people find new jobs or new businesses.

# Spending, Taxing, and the Deficit

## SOS Spending

*Arriving at a Win-Win Budget*
Each allocation in Table 1.4 is arrived at by: (1) multiplying the percentages in the goal columns by the neutral, conservative, or liberal weights, (2) summing across the products, (3) dividing the sum by the total of the appropriate weights to obtain a weighted average allocation percentage, and then (4) multiplying the total budget of $200 by that allocation percentage.

The super-optimum budget is $243 since that is the minimum amount which will allow for a bigger allocation than the best expectations of both the conservatives ($112 + $1 to the police) and the liberals ($129 +$1 to the courts).

**Table 1.4   SOS Spending**

| Budget Categories | C Goal Crime Reduction. | L Goal Fair Procedure. | N Allocation Wts = 2&2 | C Allocation Wts = 3&1 | L Allocation Wts = 1&3 | SOS Allocation |
|---|---|---|---|---|---|---|
| **C Item** Money for police. | 2 (67%) | 1 (25%) | $92 (46%) | (X) $112 (56%) | $71 (35%) | X+1 $113 (46%) |
| **L Item** Money for courts. | 1 (33%) | 3 (75%) | $108 (54%) | $88 (44%) | (Y) $129 (65%) | Y+1 $130 (54%) |
| **TOTALS** | 3 | 4 | $200 | $200 | $200 | $243 |

*Obtaining a Bigger Budget or Using the Present Budget*
*More Efficiently*

The next step would be to analyze various ways of increasing the budget from $200 to $243, and then taking the best combination of those in light of various criteria. There is an alternative approach to increasing the budget to a SOS amount that satisfies the best initial expectations of both liberals and conservatives. The alternative involves satisfying conservatives by enabling the police and the courts to be more efficient in crime reduction so they will not need so much money.

The police can be more efficient by being more visible such as covering highway policing with their red lights continuously flashing. The courts can be more efficient in crime reduction by using better screening and reporting with regard to those who have been released on bail prior to trial.

The alternative also involves satisfying liberals by enabling the police and the courts to be more efficient in using fair procedures. The police can be more efficient and effective by giving a summons to appear in many arrest cases rather than booking and jailing the suspect. The courts can be more efficient and effective regarding fair procedure by allowing jurors to view each day's trial on videotape. This helps clarify matters that might otherwise be forgotten. Jurors can also be allowed to take notes, ask questions of judges and the lawyers, and receive some training before becoming jurors.

## SOS Taxing

*Conservative and Liberal Alternatives*

The conservative position on tax sources tends to emphasize consumption taxes that are roughly equal across the general public. The liberal position tends to emphasize income taxes that bear more heavily on those with greater ability to pay.

Conservatives tend to emphasize taxes on consumption–such as the sales tax or the value added tax. Liberals tend to emphasize taxes on income especially progressive income taxes where the rates are higher on higher incomes.

**Table 1.5   Tax Sources**

| | GOALS | |
| ALTERNATIVES | Conservative<br>Stimulating investment. | Liberal<br>Ability to pay. |
| --- | --- | --- |
| **Conservative**<br>Sales tax. | + | − |
| **Liberal**<br>Income tax. | − | + |
| **Neutral**<br>Other or both. | 0 | 0 |
| **SOS or Win-Win**<br>Decrease tax rates, but<br>increase taxes with lots of<br>well-placed subsidies. | ++ | ++ |

The neutral position is to have both sales taxes and income taxes, but with the sales tax rates lower than conservatives advocate and the income tax rates lower than liberals advocate.

### Conservative and Liberal Goals

A key conservative goal is to stimulate investment. A key liberal goal is to stimulate consumption and to take into consideration the equity goal of ability to pay.

Both conservatives and liberals recognize the need for some tax money to support the government activities they like. The super-optimum solution therefore is not to abolish all taxes. That would be undesirable to both conservatives and liberals if it means abolishing the government activities they endorse. Likewise, the neutral position may result in a decrease in the government activities endorsed by conservatives and those endorsed by liberals.

### Relations between Alternatives and Goals

Sales taxes score low on consumption and ability to pay, whereas income taxes score higher. On the matter of stimulating investment, one can argue that relying on sales taxes rather than income taxes frees up more income for investment purposes. An income tax lends itself to giving tax credits in order to stimulate investment.

Regardless of how the different taxes are scored on the two goals, there does tend to be a tradeoff. Reliance on income taxes generally does better on ability to pay than on stimulating investment. That, however, depends on the extent to which the income tax provides for meaningful credits. Likewise, reliance on sales taxes generally does worse on ability to pay than on facilitating investment.

### The Win-Win Alternative

The SOS alternative involves substantially decreasing both kinds of tax rates while at the same time increasing the total tax revenue by increasing the GNP tax base. That can be partly done by well-placed tax breaks and subsidies to encourage greater national productivity.

A SOS alternative would do well on both goals. That kind of alternative might involve a combination of both taxes, but accompanied by well-placed subsidies and tax credits to stimulate increased productivity. The tax credits could also include an earned-income payment for those who are regularly working but not earning very much income and thus don't have the ability to pay high taxes.

## The Deficit

### Dealing with the Deficit

A statement of the conservative goal might be to have a strong national defense and to stimulate investment through low taxes on the relatively rich. A fuller statement of the liberal goal might be to have strong domestic policies like education and housing and to stimulate consumption through low taxes on the relative poor.

The SOS involves a reduction of taxes in the form of tax breaks designed to stimulate greater productivity. Likewise, the SOS involves an increase in spending in the form of well-placed subsidies designed to stimulate greater productivity. The increased productivity means an increased gross national product which means an increased base on which to apply the national tax rate. Thus, the tax rate can drop and still bring in increased tax revenue and thereby have more money available for government spending including defense, domestic policies, deficit reduction, and more well-placed subsidies.

## A Balanced Budget Amendment

A related issue is whether there should be an amendment to the Constitution that requires the federal budget to be balanced each year with federal spending no higher than federal tax revenue.

Conservatives endorse the amendment to keep down federal spending which is considered too liberal, especially if an exception is made for defense spending. They would also like a requirement of 60 percent congressional approval for tax increases.

Liberals oppose the amendment because they want to allow for federal spending to fight unemployment and to promote economic growth. If those considerations are covered, they would endorse a prohibition on deficit spending since deficits lead to government borrowing which boosts interest rates. Such increases interfere with consumer purchasing and business expansion.

The neutral position is to have a balanced budget amendment, but with exceptions. The conservatives especially want an exception for a declared war or a joint resolution relating to military action. Liberals want an exception for high unemployment or at least an

**Table 1.6    Deficit**

| | GOALS | |
| --- | --- | --- |
| **ALTERNATIVES** | **Conservative**<br>Defense and<br>investment. | **Liberal**<br>Domestic programs and<br>consumption. |
| **Conservative**<br>1. Decrease domestic spending.<br>2. Increase taxes on poor. | + | − |
| **Liberal**<br>1. Decrease defense spending.<br>2. Increase taxes on rich. | − | + |
| **Neutral**<br>1. Decrease spending on both.<br>2. Increase taxes on both. | 0 | 0 |
| **SOS or Win-Win**<br>1. Increase spending.<br>2. Decrease taxes. | ++ | ++ |

exception when 60 percent of Congress votes for an increase in the national debt.

A SOS alternative would be to promote economic growth through training, new technologies, competition, exports, government capital, and other means. Growth in the GNP allows for a reduction in income tax rates with an increase in tax revenue. It also allows for a reduction in spending for welfare, with increased spending for economic growth activities. Such growth can mean increases in both profits and wages.

What may be needed is an economic growth amendment that requires or recommends the federal government to promote at least 3 percent economic growth per year. The amendment can mandate the establishment of a quasi-public Consortium for Economic Growth. Its governing board could consist of three representatives from the National Association of Manufacturers and the U.S. Chamber of Commerce, three representatives from the AFL-CIO, and three representatives from the Senate, House, and the presidency. It could have a substantial appropriation for encouraging economic growth activities.

# Organizing the Economy

### Alternative Ways of Relating the Government to the Economy

Socialism refers to government ownership and public policy designed to facilitate equality of income and wealth. Capitalism refers to private ownership with no public policy designed to facilitate equality of income, wealth, and opportunity. One could conceivably talk in terms of four policies: (1) private ownership and no equality, (2) private ownership and equality, (3) government ownership and no equality, and (4) government ownership and equality. The two elements of capitalism (private ownership and inequality) do tend to go together, and likewise with the two elements of socialism (public ownership and equality).

One can have democratic or dictatorial capitalism and democratic or dictatorial socialism, depending on whether there are universal voting rights, and minority political rights. One can have responsive or non-responsive capitalism and responsive or non-responsive socialism. Responsiveness in this context refers to being responsive to consumers and workers. Socialism is traditionally thought of as being more responsive to consumers and workers.

## Government versus Private Ownership and Operation

The SOS alternative of contracting out to private operation can even apply to public schools, post offices, and municipal transportation. In former socialistic countries, it can apply also to contracting out government-owned factories and land.

The contracting out does not have to be to only one private entrepreneur. The two most qualified lowest bidders can both receive contracts for different geographical areas, sectors of the industry, or other aspects of the contract in order to encourage competition.

Productivity and the liberal goals can be further increased through appropriate government incentives by way of well-placed tax credits

### Table 1.7 Ownership and Operation

| | GOALS | |
| --- | --- | --- |
| **ALTERNATIVES** | **Conservative**<br>High productivity. | **Liberal**<br>Equity. |
| **Conservative**<br>Government ownership<br>and operation (socialism). | + | – |
| **Liberal**<br>Private ownership and<br>operation (capitalism). | – | + |
| **Neutral**<br>Some government and<br>some private. | **0** | **0** |
| **SOS or Win-Win**<br>1. 100% government<br>   owned and 100%<br>   private operation.<br>2. 100% private with<br>   government incentives. | ++ | ++ |

and subsidies. That goes beyond what can be achieved by way of government ownership or control combined with contracting out to private operation.

Workplace quality, environmental protection, and consumer protection are not necessarily promoted by government ownership. The socialist steel mills in Poland were a good example of poor workplace quality under socialism. The socialistic TVA in the United States was a good example of poor environmental protection under socialism. Government-owned power companies having monopoly control are good examples of the lack of consumer protection under socialism.

All those goals can be better achieved by requiring them as part of the contract when contracting out. That is likely to produce greater compliance than traditional government regulation. The threat of not having the contract renewed but instead having it go to a competing company can generate greater compliance. That is better than relying on the supposed altruism of managers of government factories who are not rewarded or punished for complying with goals. The government can provide further incentives by way of well-placed subsidies and tax credits to supplement the liberal contract provisions in the contracting out.

## Competition as a Key Factor

The conservative alternative of an unregulated marketplace may lead to only one or a few firms dominating most industries. That arrangement may be profitable in the short run, although contrary to low prices. The liberal alternative of government ownership or tight regulation tends to mean a government monopoly or stifled private enterprise. That means reduced business profits, although it might mean artificially low prices to satisfy consumers as voters. The mixed economy scores in the middle on both business profits and low prices.

The SOS alternative may draw upon the stimulus to innovation and efficiency of private profit making. The SOS alternative may encourage competition through well-placed seed money and other competition facilitators. Doing so results in lower prices through a

**Table 1.8   Competition**

| | GOALS | |
|---|---|---|
| **ALTERNATIVES** | **Conservative**<br>Business profits. | **Liberal**<br>Low prices. |
| **Conservative**<br>Marketplace (monopoly). | + | − |
| **Liberal**<br>Government ownership or<br>tight regulation<br>(monopoly). | − | + |
| **Neutral**<br>Some of both (mixed<br>economy). | 0 | 0 |
| **SOS or Win-Win**<br>Stimulate competition<br>through well-placed<br>subsidies. | ++ | ++ |

competitive marketplace, rather than through a monopolistic one or through artificial price constraints.

The marketplace is associated with capitalism. It may not be associated with competition if the marketplace leads to monopolies or firms working together to decrease competition. Regulation or government ownership is associated with socialism. It is even more likely to lead to monopoly, but monopoly in the hands of the state rather than private enterprise. The marketplace may lead to better business profits than regulation does. Regulation may lead to better consumer prices than the marketplace does.

A SOS alternative is competition which is likely to lead to even better total business profits than the marketplace, although not necessarily better profits for each firm. Competition is likely to lead to better consumer prices and quality of products than regulation. Competition can be stimulated through laws that (1) require licensing of patents and facilities, (2) lower tariffs to increase international competition, (3) provide seed money to get new businesses established or expanded to make an industry more competitive, and (4) require leasing of networks of electricity, telephone, and cable television.

## Equity in Socialism and Capitalism

Capitalism differs from socialism mainly in terms of government versus private ownership and operation of the major means of production and distribution. Capitalism also differs from socialism with regard to the extent to which inequality of income and wealth is allowed.

Under pure capitalism, there are no limits to the degree of permissible inequality in income and wealth. Under socialism, there are progressive income taxes and inheritance taxes designed to promote a substantial amount of equality in income and wealth.

Capitalism justifies economic inequality as a stimulus to increased productivity. The theory is people will work harder and be more innovative in order to receive the rewards of greater income and wealth.

Socialism justifies having greater income equality as the fair or equitable thing to do, especially in the context of providing a minimum floor regarding food, shelter, and clothing to the poor.

**Table 1.9   Equity**

|  | GOALS | |
| --- | --- | --- |
| **ALTERNATIVES** | **Conservative**<br>Productivity. | **Liberal**<br>Equity (minimum floor). |
| **Conservative**<br>Income inequality<br>(capitalism). | + | − |
| **Liberal**<br>Income equality<br>(socialism). | − | + |
| **Neutral**<br>In between. | 0 | 0 |
| **SOS or Win-Win**<br>1. Negative income tax or<br>   earned income credit.<br>2. Tax breaks for upgrad-<br>   ing skills. | ++ | ++ |

A SOS alternative that does well on both the conservative and liberal goals involves allowing considerable inequality in income and wealth but providing a minimum floor. That can be done through a negative income tax whereby people who are below that minimum level receive a payment from the Internal Revenue Service instead of paying to the IRS.

A better approach is to emphasize the earned income credit whereby the people below a minimum level who work are rewarded by receiving an IRS payment. Those who do not work receive public aid and assistance in finding a job. The SOS may also provide tax breaks and subsidies for upgrading individual skills in order to increase one's productivity.

## Political-Economic Competition and Prosperity

Table 1.10 only includes industrial nations. A separate table could be made for developing nations. Among industrialized nations, those that provide for competition in politics and economics have more prosperity than those who do not provide for competition in both activities. Industrialized nations that provide for competition in only one of the two activities are likely to have middling prosperity, although competition in politics may be more important to prosperity than competition in economics.

Table 1.10 is mainly designed to relate political and economic competition as key causes in prosperity. One could also interpret it as tending to show that countries that have economic competition are more likely to have political competition and vice versa.

One could also interpret Table 1.10 as tending to show that industrialized nations are more likely to have a higher standard of living than non-industrialized nations regardless of political and economic competition. Another conclusion that the table generates is that whether a country has capitalistic private ownership or socialistic government ownership is virtually irrelevant to prosperity in comparison to political-economic competition and industrialization.

**Table 1.10  Political-Economic Competition and Prosperity**

| | Competition (Causal Variable) | |
| | No — In politics and economics. | Yes — In politics and economics. |
| --- | --- | --- |
| **Prosperity or High Standard of Living** (Effect Variable) | | West Germany (Capitalism)  Sweden (Socialism) |
| | East Germany (Socialism)  Spain Pre-1980 (Capitalism) | |

# Other Economic Issues

The economic issues that we have discussed all deal with the economy as a whole. They are macro-economic issues, as contrasted to issues that deal with an individual firm or with land, labor, and capital as the major factors of production. Sometimes government policy is added as a fourth factor. We consider government policy to be present in discussing how to promote effectiveness, efficiency, and equity in using the other three factors and other societal resources.

## Land

A key tradeoff issue dealing with land or natural resources in the United States is the alleged conflict between high farm production and high farm income. The United Sates may be the only country in the world where farmers have been encouraged to produce less in order to create artificially high prices. In other countries, farmers are encouraged to grow more in order to feed the population and have crops for export. A win-win solution that was recently adopted under the title of "Freedom to Farm" allows farmers to produce all they want in anticipation that the world market will be able to absorb their extra production.

Unfortunately, when subsidies were abolished for setting aside land, the Asian and Russian markets decreased their ability to buy. The problem is not the lack of demand, or that American farm products are high-priced. There is plenty of demand, and American farmers are highly efficient. The problem seems to be that when China or Russia want to buy wheat, they are likely to buy it from Australia, Argentina, or Canada because they can afford Australia, Argentina, and Canadian dollars more than they can afford U.S. dollars. The U.S. dollar is high-priced compared, for example, to the Canadian dollar.

The American government drives up the price of the dollar whenever it seeks to sell U.S. Treasury bonds in order to borrow from new lenders to pay off old lenders. We could reduce the national debt (like we have reduced the annual deficit) through economic growth, which provides increased government revenue and decreased welfare spending. The price of the dollar would then go down. As a result, farmers could sell more goods overseas, and so could all other American producers. That would be a super win-win for America and the consumers of American products.

## Labor

A good example of a win-win labor policy relates to the minimum wage. Whenever there is a suggestion of raising the minimum wage, management talks about having to lay off workers whose families will starve. Labor talks about families already starving because the minimum wage is not a living wage. The usual result, however, is a compromise in which both sides are allowing for some alleged starvation. A win-win solution is needed whereby management, for example, could pay less than four monetary units an hour and labor could receive more than five monetary units per hour. That involves minimum-wage vouchers. These vouchers are worth $1. They are given to unemployed workers, or to employers to enable them to pay workers $4 an hour plus a $1 voucher that can be cashed at the bank.

To receive this $1 subsidy, the employer must agree to provide on-the-job training to bring the worker's skills up to a $5 an hour level within six months. Likewise, to receive this $1 subsidy, the worker must agree to participate in the on-the-job training and to pass the final exam. This is a win-win for management and workers. It is also a win-win for society because it saves tax money that might otherwise go to unemployment compensation, public aid, food stamps, public housing, anti-crime expenses, Medicaid, and other services for the unemployed. Society also benefits because these newly employed people pay taxes that support productivity-increasing public policy. The workers are also better role models for their children and grandchildren.

Workers who already work for the firm would also be eligible to take the on-the-job training in order to be in the voucher program to increase their wages above the minimum wage. The voucher program is, however, especially beneficial to the economy if it enables unemployed people to work at the minimum wage or above when they otherwise would not be hired. This kind of wage voucher could also apply to elderly workers, disabled workers, and others to temporarily fill the gap between what employers are willing to pay and what might be considered a living wage.

**Capital**

A win-win example dealing with capital is the stock market. It is a big source of capital in the United States, although Japan relies more heavily on bank savings and the tax-supported Ministry of International Trade and Industry. A conflict of interest in stock brokerage is between small investors and the middlemen brokers who facilitate obtaining capital for big firms. The problem is that those who sell stocks and bonds would like to get as big a cut of their sales as possible. Those who buy stocks and bonds would like to pay as small a commission as possible.

Commissions could increase to make both sellers and buyers simultaneously happy by changing the present payment system. The current system pays sellers a percentage of what they get the investor to buy. This inherently encourages brokers to encourage investors to buy more than they possibly should, and to buy more of certain shares that pay high commissions. A win-win alternative would be to pay on the basis of good performance. That way a broker would get a substantial percentage of the dividends within the first five years, or whatever percentage and time period is negotiated. The broker could also get a substantial percentage of the increase in the value of stock upon resale. Such an arrangement could enable good brokers to make a lot more money, which would also benefit the stock buyers. A minimum fee could be provided on the basis of hours worked.

There is a need for more performance pay in all fields of the private and public sectors so as to enable both sellers and consumers to come out ahead of their best initial expectations. Total profits of stock sellers could also be increased if banks were allowed to sell stock. The competition would allow qualified banks to make a legitimate profit that they are currently denied. The stock buyers would also benefit from the competition. Indeed, stimulated competition and the structured or channeled profit motive may be the two most important concepts in win-win economic policy.

# Chapter 2

# International Prosperity

## International Exchange of Goods

### Improving International Competitiveness

The conservative position (as indicated in the Bush administration) has been to emphasize that government regulation increases business expenses and thereby reduces international competitiveness.

The liberal position (as indicated in the Carter administration) has been to emphasize the need to lower tariffs, break up monopolies, and

**Table 2.1  International Competitiveness**

| ALTERNATIVES | GOALS | |
| --- | --- | --- |
| | Conservative<br>Business profits. | Liberal<br>Labor and consumers. |
| **Conservative**<br>Decrease government regulations. | + | − |
| **Liberal**<br>1. Lower tariffs.<br>2. Anti-trust action.<br>3. Labor-management teamwork. | − | + |
| **Neutral**<br>Keep as is. | 0 | 0 |
| **SOS or Win-Win**<br>1. Government investment in technology diffusion.<br>2. Upgrading of skills. | ++ | ++ |

encourage more labor-management teamwork.

The neutral position has been to avoid substantial changes in regulation, tariffs, and other such controversies.

The SOS alternative (as indicated by some elements in the Clinton administration) is to emphasize government investment in technological diffusion and the upgrading of skills. Doing so is capable of increasing the profits of business and the wages of labor. It can also result in better products at lower prices for both domestic and international markets.

## Evaluating Alternative Positions on Tariffs

On the issue of tariffs, conservatives who believe in free competitive markets both internationally and domestically tend to favor low tariffs. Likewise, so do liberals who have an internationalistic orientation and who recognize the mutual benefits from buying overseas goods that have low prices, high quality, and the ability to stimulate competitive activity on the part of American firms.

On the other hand, conservatives who support monopolistic American businesses with their unreasonable profits are in favor of high tariffs. Likewise, pro-union liberals who do not want foreign competition are also in favor of high tariffs.

Traditionally, American conservatives have supported high tariffs, and American liberals have supported low tariffs. The new SOS position is to support low or no tariffs, especially to stimulate worldwide competition to the long-term benefit of more efficient production and more prosperous consumption.

The object is to develop plans for well-placed subsidies and tax breaks that will enable the United States to compete effectively for world market shares without the interference and mutual downgrading of high tariffs. That especially means encouraging the adoption and diffusion of new technologies, and the upgrading of worker skills to be able to put the new technologies to good use. The result, at least in the long run, is likely to be high business profits, high workers' wages, low consumer prices, high consumer quality, and lower tax rates in view of the increased GNP as a tax base.

## Table 2.2   Tariffs

| | GOALS | |
|---|---|---|
| **ALTERNATIVES** | **Conservative** <br> High profits. | **Liberal** <br> High wages. |
| **Conservative** <br> 1. Pro-business conservatives, high tariffs. <br> 2. Free world market conservatives, low tariffs. | + | − |
| **Liberal** <br> 1. Pro-union liberals, high tariffs. <br> 2. Internationalist liberals, low tariffs. | − | + |
| **Neutral** <br> Middling tariffs. | 0 | 0 |
| **SOS or Win-Win** <br> Well-placed subsidies and tax breaks. | ++ | ++ |

## Getting Japan and Other Countries to Reduce Tariffs

On this policy problem, conservatives and liberals have the same general goal of reducing foreign tariffs. In order to be a controversy, there must be a difference of opinion as to the best alternative to use in achieving that goal.

The conservative position tends to emphasize retaliatory raising of tariffs as the most effective way of reducing foreign tariffs. The liberal position tends to emphasize negotiation and bargaining without explicit threats, but with promises of mutual tariff reduction. The neutral position is some of both.

There is a controversy here because conservatives and liberals perceive differently the relations between the alternatives and their shared goal. The conservative perception is that threats will do well, but conciliatory negotiation will not do so well. The liberals perceive that negotiating is more likely to do well, and that threats will not do so well.

**Table 2.3    Getting Reduced Tariffs**

|  | GOALS | |
| --- | --- | --- |
| **ALTERNATIVES** | **Conservative**<br>1. Reducing foreign tariffs.<br>2. Conservative perception. | **Liberal**<br>1. Reducing foreign tariffs.<br>2. Liberal perception. |
| **Conservative**<br>Threaten retaliatory tariff increase. | + | − |
| **Liberal**<br>Negotiating mutual tariff reduction. | − | + |
| **Neutral**<br>Some of both. | 0 | 0 |
| **SOS or Win-Win**<br>1. Subsidy to bypass foreign tariffs.<br>2. Positive incentives. | ++ | ++ |

In calculating the total scores, conservatives give more weight to their perceptions than to the perceptions of liberals. Likewise, liberals give more weight to their own perceptions. On a 1-3 scale, each group gives a weight or multiplier of about 3 to its own perceptions, and a weight of about 1 to the other group's perceptions.

The super-optimum solution should be perceived as doing better than the neutral alternative by both conservatives and liberals. That enables the SOS to score higher on the conservative totals than the conservative alternative, and higher on the liberal totals than the liberal alternative.

The SOS might include a subsidy to enable efficient domestic producers to bypass the foreign tariff. For example, if U.S. rice producers are unable to sell to Japanese consumers because there is a $1 tariff on each bushel of rice, then it might be worthwhile for the U.S. government to subsidize the rice farmers to the extent of $.90 per bushel. This may be enough to enable them to make a profit in spite of the Japanese tariff. It would be worth it to the U.S. government if the subsidy keeps a lot of people employed and brings in a large amount of income to add to the GNP. Otherwise, the subsidy may not be cost-effective. Such a subsidy is more likely to make sense where the Japanese government is under intense pressure from a politically powerful Japanese industry to retain the tariff.

The SOS can also include positive incentives. An example might be that the United States will agree to share in developing or marketing a new technology with Japan in return for a lowering of the tariff on rice. That positive incentive may be enough to stimulate the Japanese government to find a different way to subsidize Japanese rice farmers, rather than providing them with a tariff which hurts Japanese food consumption.

## The North American Free Trade Agreement

U.S. exporters and investors are helped by free trade with Mexico and other places because: (1) Mexicans can buy more U.S. products if there are no Mexican tariffs artificially raising the price of American products, (2) Mexicans can buy more U.S. products if they have more income as a result of working in factories that have expanded as a result of American capital, and (3) U.S. investors can make money and add to the U.S. GNP by investing in Mexican factories which are now able to export better to the United States because U.S. tariffs have been dropped.

U.S. consumers are helped by free trade with Mexico and other places because: (1) they can buy products made in Mexico at lower prices because they no longer have a U.S. tariff artificially raising the prices, (2) they can benefit from low prices that should result from decreased labor expenses associated with some products made in Mexico, possibly stimulated with American capital, and (3) U.S. consumers include business firms that buy producer goods less expensively from Mexico and thereby make American firms more internationally competitive.

U.S. firms and workers who are not sufficiently competitive would be hurt by the NAFTA agreement, but this can be minimized by: (1) retraining workers and firms so they can be more competitive in their old products or new products, (2) sign agreements with

Mexico that require upgrading of labor standards in Mexico, and (3) disrupted workers and firms may benefit from the increased prosperity of the United States as a result of more exporting, better overseas investing, and better buys for U.S. consumers.

Mexicans can benefit in the same ways as Americans by just substituting for the goal columns Mexican exporters and investors, non-competitive Mexican firms and workers, and Mexican consumers.

The opponents of NAFTA are referred to in Table 2.4 as conservatives and the advocates are referred to as liberals. That is done partly to simplify the calculation of the totals. It is also in accordance with the fact that conservatives have traditionally been in favor of high tariffs, although in recent years that is less true than from about 1800 through the 1930s.

**Table 2.4   NAFTA**

|  | GOALS | |
| --- | --- | --- |
| **ALTERNATIVES** | **Conservative**<br>Non-competitive U.S.<br>firms and workers. | **Liberal**<br>U.S. consumers. |
| **Conservative**<br>1. Opponents.<br>2. Labor unions and weak<br>    business firms. | + | − |
| **Liberal**<br>1. Advocates.<br>2. Intellectual liberals.<br>3. Most business interests. | − | + |
| **Neutral**<br>Middling. | 0 | 0 |
| **SOS or Win-Win**<br>1. Free trade.<br>2. Retraining.<br>3. Side agreements.<br>4. Expanding economy. | ++ | ++ |

# Exchange of People

## U.S. Immigration Policy

Saying that conservatives favor more restrictions on immigration than liberals do is not quite true. Those who favor restrictions do tend to be people who emphasize racial purity, but also working people who resist immigrant competition. Likewise, those who favor relaxing restrictions may be liberals who want to provide opportunities to minority people from developing nations, but also conservative business people who welcome cheap labor.

Greatly restricting immigration could mean having very low quotas for different parts of the world. It could mean requiring jobs in advance or having relatives in the United States. Mildly restricting immigration means allowing much higher immigration figures and not requiring jobs in advance. Greatly restricting immigration tends to avoid unemployment of American workers at least in the short run. In the long run, ambitious immigrants may enhance the economy so as to provide more employment opportunities. Mildly restricting immigration welcomes ambitious people, although it may also welcome people who could be a drain on the economy.

A SOS solution that enables all sides to come out ahead might emphasize jobs for displaced workers. That would mean special programs to upgrade the skills of workers in areas where there is high immigration. A SOS solution might also emphasize ambition criteria in determining who is eligible to come to the United States. Such criteria might favor those who are themselves seeking higher education or educational opportunities for their children. Such criteria might exclude people who have a high probability of being on public aid, as indicated by various predictive characteristics including responses to interviews. If an immigrant does commit a crime or wrongly applies for public aid, then he can be sent back with both a free ticket and a suspended sentence to be reinstituted if he breaks the terms of the sentence.

**Table 2.5    Immigration**

| | GOALS | |
| --- | --- | --- |
| **ALTERNATIVES** | **Conservative**<br>Avoid unemployment. | **Liberal**<br>Welcome ambitious people. |
| **Conservative**<br>Greatly restrict immigration. | + | − |
| **Liberal**<br>Mildly restrict immigration. | − | + |
| **Neutral**<br>In between. | 0 | 0 |
| **SOS or Win-Win**<br>Jobs for displaced workers and ambition criteria. | ++ | ++ |

## International Refugees

International refugees are people who have been forced out of their nations by war or natural disasters and are waiting to return or to go elsewhere. Emigrants are people who are voluntarily leaving their homes and going to other nations where they are considered immigrants.

The conservative position is to keep refugees out partly to protect national purity, but also to avoid competition for jobs. The liberal position is to let refugees in partly to help them, out of sympathy, but also in recognition that they may provide useful labor and innovative ideas through themselves or their children. The compromise is to let some refugees in, but on a selective basis with restrictions.

The SOS solution might be to upgrade the skills of international refugees through organized international efforts, possibly under the direction of the United Nations. With greater skills, the refugees might be more acceptable to both conservatives and liberals, given their increased productivity and ability to enhance the economies of the countries to which they go.

**Table 2.6   Refugees**

| ALTERNATIVES | GOALS | |
| --- | --- | --- |
| | **Conservative** Protect national purity. | **Liberal** Promote quality of life of refugees and society. |
| **Conservative** Refugees out. | + | − |
| **Liberal** Refugees in. | − | + |
| **Neutral** In between. | 0 | 0 |
| **SOS or Win-Win** Upgrade skills. | ++ | ++ |

## Volunteerism in Technical Assistance

Hiring expensive, experienced technicians for technical assistance programs may be highly effective in producing the results desired by liberals, but it is contrary to the cost savings desired by conservatives. Relying on the initiative of idealistic volunteers like missionaries may not be so effective, but it does save costs. The neutral compromise is to have volunteers in the field, but salaried professionals in U.S. government agencies like the Peace Corps.

The alternatives can be referred to as Position 1 and Position 2, rather than as conservative or liberal. Position 1 (relying on volunteers) is conservative in having low cost, but not conservative in producing pro-business results. Position 2 (relying on paid professionals) is liberal because of generous spending, but not liberal in results in being pro-labor or pro-consumer.

The SOS alternative might be to work through professional associations. For example, engineering associations would actively recruit engineering volunteers. Lawyer associations would recruit lawyer volunteers, and so on. One would thereby get experts for the price of idealistic volunteers.

**Table 2.7  Volunteerism**

| | GOALS | |
|---|---|---|
| **ALTERNATIVES** | **Conservative**<br>Cost saving and<br>efficiency. | **Liberal**<br>Effectiveness. |
| **Conservative**<br>Buy technical assistance. | + | − |
| **Liberal**<br>Rely on volunteers. | − | + |
| **Neutral**<br>Volunteerism agencies,<br>e.g., Peace Corps. | 0 | 0 |
| **SOS or Win-Win**<br>Work through<br>professional associations. | ++ | ++ |

# Exchange of Factories

## Foreign Factories in the United States

The basic issue here is whether encouraging foreign factories to locate in the United States provides more benefits than costs in terms of the national employment and income.

The benefits mainly consist of providing jobs for Americans who work in the factories. The costs mainly consist of increasing the competitiveness of foreign firms to take away American customers from American firms and thereby decrease employment in those American firms.

Encouragement of foreign factories could consist of tax benefits and subsidies or simply being allowed in on an equal basis with American factories.

The issue is similar to the issue of allowing foreign products into the United States on an equal basis with American products, meaning no tariffs or other restrictions. Doing so is good for the American consumer. It also stimulates American business to operate more efficiently and facilitates their being able to sell overseas.

**Table 2.8    Foreign Factories**

| ALTERNATIVES | GOALS | |
| --- | --- | --- |
| | Conservative<br>U.S. profits. | Liberal<br>U.S. jobs. |
| **Conservative**<br>No encouragement for<br>foreign factories in United<br>States. | + | − |
| **Liberal**<br>Substantial encourage-<br>ment. | − | + |
| **Neutral**<br>In between. | 0 | 0 |
| **SOS or Win-Win**<br>Improve competitiveness<br>of U.S. firms. | ++ | ++ |

In addition to the same consumer benefits of having tariffs on foreign products, encouraging foreign factories provides Americans job opportunities. It does, however, increase foreign competitiveness by reducing transportation costs. It may also make American consumers more willing to buy knowing that the products have been made in the United States, even though the firm is headquartered elsewhere.

There is currently division within the Clinton administration on this issue, but those in favor of encouraging foreign factories are winning on the grounds that there is a net increase in jobs and other benefits.

The Clinton compromise may result in a net increase in jobs, but (at least in the short run) it also results in a decrease in the profits of competing American business firms. The net increase in jobs though may result in an overall increase in the GNP, more than offsetting the decrease in profits.

A SOS solution would seek to increase both U.S. jobs and U.S. profits if possible. Providing encouragement, or at least equal access, scores reasonably well on jobs. To have a policy that also scores reasonably well on profits, it would be helpful to have an organized program to aid American businesses that are being subjected to increased competition by the foreign factories locating in the United States. That does not mean aid in the form of a bailout or handout. It means seed money or investment money to improve their technologies and upgrade the skills of their workers so they can be truly more competitive with both foreign factories in the United States and overseas.

A SOS solution might also provide temporary investment money to enable American firms to build factories overseas to be closer to foreign markets. Doing so provides jobs for foreign workers. There may still be a net gain to the U.S. GNP if the foreign sales bring in U.S. income that more than offsets the loss of jobs to foreign workers. This may be especially so if U.S. factories overseas are supplemented by an expansion of related factories in the United States in order to supply those overseas factories with parts and related products.

### U.S. Factories Going Abroad

The problem here is whether there should be any restrictions or encouragement relating to American companies locating factories abroad.

The conservative position is no restrictions. The liberal position is to prohibit U.S. firms from locating abroad where doing so involves going below American fair labor standards as in the Fair Labor Standards Act (FLSA) statutes. A compromise position would be to allow companies to locate factories abroad with a relaxing of the FLSA standards, but still making them at least partly applicable.

Conservatives are interested in promoting business profits. Liberals are interested in promoting employment for American labor under good wages and working conditions.

Business profits are promoted if an overseas factory has closer access to customers, raw materials, or skilled inexpensive labor. Those profits become part of an increased U.S. national income. Locating factories overseas can also facilitate selling abroad which helps in the trade deficit whereby we would otherwise be buying substantially more than we would be selling. The U.S. factories operating abroad may be producing products especially for the American market which can be sold at a lower price to Americans than if the products were made in factories located in the United States where labor and resources might be more expensive.

The disruption to American employment can be reduced in various ways. One is to have free trade agreements with foreign countries whereby they agree to establish and enforce fair labor standards on American companies and other companies. Another approach is to subsidize the upgrading of relevant American labor skills to make American labor more competitive, or to enable displaced workers to go into other higher paying jobs. A third approach might be to place an import tax on goods made with unfair labor standards by U.S.-owned companies or others. The companies could avoid the tax by upgrading their foreign labor standards.

That three-part package could be considered as moving in a super-optimum direction where both business and labor come out ahead. In the long run, the free movement of goods and factories across

**Table 2.9   U.S. Factories Abroad**

| | GOALS | |
|---|---|---|
| **ALTERNATIVES** | **Conservative**<br>Business profits. | **Liberal**<br>Good working conditions. |
| **Conservative**<br>No constraints. | + | − |
| **Liberal**<br>1. Prohibit U.S. firms<br>  abroad from violating<br>  fair labor standards. | − | + |
| **Neutral**<br>1. No free trade<br>  agreement without fair<br>  labor standards. | 0 | 0 |
| **SOS or Win-Win**<br>1. Free trade agreements<br>  with guarantees.<br>2. Import tax on goods<br>  made with unfair labor<br>  standards. | ++ | ++ |

international boundaries would have the effect of raising the national income of all the countries involved, thereby producing a more general super-optimum solution.

The problem of U.S. factories going abroad especially relates to factories moving to developing nations like Mexico or Southeast Asia. A partial justification is that doing so helps those developing nations to build up their economies so they can become better customers for American products, better suppliers to American producers and consumers, and better outlets for American investment. For example, wages earned by Mexican workers in U.S. factories located in Mexico can be an important part of the ability of Mexico to buy American goods.

# General Exchange Facilitators

## Dollar Exchange Rates

A high dollar value means that $1 will buy many units of the currencies of other countries. A low dollar value means that $1 will buy relatively few units of the currencies of other countries.

**Table 2.10 Dollar Exchange Rates**

|  | GOALS | |
|---|---|---|
| **ALTERNATIVES** | **Conservative**<br>Buy from other countries. | **Liberal**<br>Sell to other countries. |
| **Conservative**<br>High dollar value. | + | − |
| **Liberal**<br>Low dollar value. | − | + |
| **Neutral**<br>Middle dollar value. | 0 | 0 |
| **SOS or Win-Win**<br>Improve quality and price<br>of U.S. goods. | ++ | ++ |

If the dollar has a relatively high value, then we have difficulty selling to other countries because they have to give a lot of units of their currencies in order to get a dollar. If the dollar has relatively low value, then we have difficulty buying from other countries because Americans have to give a lot of dollars in order to get the currencies of other countries.

If we concentrate on improving the quality and prices of American goods, then we can sell a lot of American goods to other countries without lowering the value of the dollar. A big effect of selling a lot more to other countries is the increase in the American national income. That enables us to have a lot more money to buy from other countries without raising the value of the dollar.

Thus, improving the quality and price of American goods through upgrading technologies and skills is a good SOS solution because it can achieve both goals of increased buying and increased selling simultaneously. This is in contrast to manipulating the dollar which increases one goal but decreases the other goal in a typical tradeoff pattern.

## International Economic Communities

The relations between each alternative and each goal in Table 2.11 can be shown on a 1-5 relations scale. A 5 means highly conducive to the goal, a 4 means mildly conducive, a 3 means neither conducive nor adverse, a 2 means mildly adverse, and a 1 means highly adverse to the goal.

The conservative goal is given a weight or multiplier of 3 by conservatives on a 1-3 scale of weights, but a weight of 1 by liberals. The liberal goal is given a weight or multiplier of 1 by conservatives, but a weight of 3 by liberals.

A single asterisk can show the alternative that wins on the liberal totals before considering the SOS alternative. It is likely to be the liberal alternative. A single asterisk can also show the alternative that wins on the conservative totals before considering the SOS alternative. It is likely to be the conservative alternative.

A double asterisk can show the alternative or alternatives that win on each total after the SOS super-optimum solution is considered. The SOS should score higher than both the former conservative winner on the conservative totals, and simultaneously higher than the former liberal winner on the liberal totals.

The international economic community scores well on the conservative goal of national identity and stature. No sovereignty is given up. Each member of the community gains some stature by being associated with a larger, more powerful body than itself. The IEC also promotes the liberal goal of quality of life in terms of jobs and consumer goods by: (1) allowing for the free flow of job applicants across international boundaries, (2) removing tariff barriers to higher consumer standards of living, and (3) providing for a better division of labor among the countries which facilitates more jobs and more consumer goods.

**Table 2.11 International Economic Communities**

| | GOALS | |
|---|---|---|
| **ALTERNATIVES** | **Conservative** National identity and stature. | **Liberal** Quality of life in terms of jobs and consumer goods. |
| **Conservative** Nationalism and separatism. | + | − |
| **Liberal** One world or world government. | − | + |
| **Neutral** Regional government. | 0 | 0 |
| **SOS or Win-Win** Economic community. | ++ | ++ |

# PART TWO

# ECONOMIC POLICY

# Section A

# Improving the Total Economy

# Chapter 3

---

# Employment and Inflation

## Employment

### SOS Analysis of Unemployment Independent of Inflation

Upgrading skills helps to make unemployed workers more employable. More important, upgrading skills increases worker productivity, which increases the GNP, national income, and national spending. The increased spending makes for more jobs.

The improved technologies also increase productivity, GNP, national income, and national spending. That also results in more jobs thereby reducing unemployment. The increased productivity makes business more profitable and results in higher wages.

Relying on the marketplace does not solve unemployment if wage rates stay high due to decreased competition as a result of unions. Likewise, prices do not fall in times of recession if businesses are not competitive.

Lowering interest rates will not result in borrowing for business expansion or durable goods when businesses are operating on reduced capacity and consumers are fearful of unemployment.

Spending more and taxing less by the government may not be politically feasible when the annual deficit and the national debt are already too high, thereby interfering with government flexibility, low interest rates, and international trade.

**Table 3.1    Unemployment Independent of Inflation**

| | GOALS | |
| | Conservative | Liberal |
| **ALTERNATIVES** | More business profits. | Higher wages. |
| --- | --- | --- |
| **Conservative**<br>1. Do nothing.<br>2. Leave marketplace.<br>3. Lower interest. | + | − |
| **Liberal**<br>1. Spend more.<br>2. Tax less. | − | + |
| **Neutral**<br>Some of both. | 0 | 0 |
| **SOS or Win-Win**<br>1. Strict merit, no<br>    seniority.<br>2. Upgrade skills.<br>3. Seniority within a<br>    range. | ++ | ++ |

## Dealing with Layoffs and Affirmative Action Simultaneously

The conservative position is to follow the usual rule in layoffs that the last people hired should be the first people laid off or fired. That means no extra consideration is given to minorities who may be disproportionately among those most recently hired.

The liberal position is to add some seniority to recently hired minority people. For example, each minority person hired could be given a few years seniority on the grounds that minority people probably should have been hired at least a few years sooner generally than when they were actually hired.

The neutral position might be to award some automatic seniority, but maybe only one year rather than a few years. Another neutral position might be to judge each case individually in terms of the age of the employee and other relevant characteristics in determining whether any additional seniority should be given.

**Table 3.2    Layoffs and Affirmative Action**

| ALTERNATIVES | GOALS | |
|---|---|---|
| | **Conservative**<br>Merit hiring and firing. | **Liberal**<br>Do something for minorities. |
| **Conservative**<br>As is, no points. | + | − |
| **Liberal**<br>Preferential non-layoffs,<br>10 years. | − | + |
| **Neutral**<br>One year. | **0** | **0** |
| **SOS or Win-Win**<br>1. Strict merit, no<br>    seniority.<br>2. Upgrade skills.<br>3. Seniority within a<br>    range. | ++ | ++ |

The SOS alternative might be to handle layoffs only or mainly on the basis of merit qualifications, rather than seniority. Doing so should appeal to the conservative emphasis on merit. It would also allow some recently hired minorities to have a better chance at being retained than if only seniority is considered.

The SOS alternative might also include a program for upgrading the skills of recently hired employees and other employees so they can score higher on merit criteria.

Another modification might be to consider seniority among employees who are within the same merit range, or to consider merit within a broadly defined seniority range. Thus merit would determine who gets laid off among all employees who have less than 10 years seniority, 10-20 years seniority, and so on.

# Inflation

## SOS Analysis of Inflation Independent of Unemployment

Upgrading skills offsets the inflation of wage rates because purchasers of labor will be getting more for their money even if the price of labor goes up.

Improving technologies (so as to improve the quality of products) offsets the inflation of price increases because consumers of products will be getting more for their money even if the prices go up.

It is not meaningful to discuss the effects of spending less and taxing more since that alternative is politically unfeasible.

Raising interest rates may reduce inflation, but with an adverse effect on business profits by making it difficult to borrow for expansion or even for regular activities. Raising interest rates may also decrease spending, increase unemployment, and thereby decrease total wages.

For those who are on fixed incomes, public policy needs to protect them against inflation by indexing their incomes to cost of living increases.

**Table 3.3    Inflation Independent of Unemployment**

| | GOALS | |
|---|---|---|
| **ALTERNATIVES** | **Conservative**<br>More business profits. | **Liberal**<br>Higher wages. |
| **Conservative**<br>Raise interest rates. | + | − |
| **Liberal**<br>Lower interest rates. | − | + |
| **Neutral**<br>Retain interest rates. | 0 | 0 |
| **SOS or Win-Win**<br>1. Increase new<br>   technologies.<br>2. Upgrade worker skills. | ++ | ++ |

**Table 3.4   Inflation and Russia**

| ALTERNATIVES | GOALS | |
| --- | --- | --- |
| | **Conservative** Fast stop to inflation. | **Liberal** Fast move to free enterprise. |
| **Conservative** Command economy (price control). | + | – |
| **Liberal** Free marketplace (hands-off). | – | + |
| **Neutral** 1. Indexing. 2. Interest rates. 3. Spending-taxing. | **0** | **0** |
| **SOS or Win-Win** Raise GNP fast by well-placed incentives. | ++ | ++ |

## Inflation and Russia, 1991

The SOS incentives are designed to stimulate: (1) better marketing, (2) more competition, and (3) more equitable distribution through vouchers for good, clothes, and housing.

# Employment and Inflation Simultaneously

## Deciding Whether to Raise or Lower Interest Rates

Table 3.5 is a highly simplified SOS table dealing with inflation and unemployment. It is simplified in the sense that it only deals with manipulating interest rates, rather than manipulating taxing and spending as well.

The government can raise or lower interest rates by: (1) changing the discount rate that is charged to banks who want to borrow from the Federal Reserve System, (2) changing the percentage or ratio of deposits that must be retained on reserve in banks, and (3) buying or selling treasury bonds in order to influence that important interest rate.

Conservatives have traditionally been more sensitive to reducing inflation than reducing unemployment in comparison to liberals, and vice versa. Conservatives have tended to identify with lenders, rather than borrowers. Liberals have tended to identify with workers, rather than employers. Conservatives increasingly recognize that businesses are borrowers and that unemployment cuts consumption. Liberals increasingly recognize that inflation hurts people on relatively fixed incomes.

For the above reasons, conservatives traditionally favor high interest rates. This is also helpful to people who have property and wealth which might lose much of its value in times of inflation. Liberals traditionally favor low interest rates, which stimulate consumption and the kind of spending that creates jobs.

Thus, we have a classic trade-off where the conservative alternative does well on the conservative goal, but not so well on the liberal goal. The liberal alternative does well on the liberal goal, but not so well on the conservative goal.

**Table 3.5    Interest Rates**

| | GOALS | |
| --- | --- | --- |
| **ALTERNATIVES** | **Conservative**<br>Reduce inflation. | **Liberal**<br>Reduce unemployment. |
| **Conservative**<br>Raise interest rates. | + | − |
| **Liberal**<br>Lower interest rates. | − | + |
| **Neutral**<br>Retain interest rates. | 0 | 0 |
| **SOS or Win-Win**<br>1. Increase new technologies.<br>2. Upgrade worker skills. | ++ | ++ |

The SOS solution might be to stimulate new technologies and upgrade workers' skills. Doing so can both reduce inflation and reduce unemployment. The connection is discussed in the notes to Table 3.7 entitled "Inflation and Unemployment." Unemployment is mainly reduced by the increased GNP and increasing spending. Inflation is mainly reduced by the increased productivity to meet the increased demand, and by the increased incomes to offset the increased prices.

Encouraging competition can be added to the SOS solution. That can be done through facilitating the entry of new business firms. Competition tends to reduce prices, which is the same as reducing inflation. Competition also tends to increase productivity and the quality of goods which increases sales, GNP, income, and spending, and thereby increases jobs and reduces unemployment.

### Evaluating Policies for Dealing with Unemployment and Inflation

Doing nothing is not likely to worsen unemployment or inflation, but it is also not likely to help.

Decreasing the money supply and increasing interest rates may decrease inflation, but increase unemployment. The same is true of decreasing government spending and increasing taxes.

The Reagonomics approach involves decreasing taxes to stimulate employment, and decreasing domestic spending to reduce inflation. The Democratic counterpart as of 1980 was to increase employment through government jobs and decrease inflation through price control.

Increasing the money supply and decreasing interests may stimulate employment, but increase inflation. The same is also true of increasing government spending and reducing taxes.

The SOS is to stimulate greater productivity through well-placed subsidies with strings attached, big money, and competent administration.

**Table 3.6    Unemployment**

|  | GOALS | |
|---|---|---|
| **ALTERNATIVES** | **Conservative**<br>1. Lower inflation to 3%.<br>2. Free enterprise. | **Liberal**<br>1. Lower unemployment to 3%.<br>2. Distribution of inflation and unemployment. |
| **Conservative**<br>1. Do nothing.<br>2. Decrease money supply & increase interest rates.<br>3. Decrease spending & increase taxes.<br>4. Decrease taxes & decrease domestic spending. | + | − |
| **Liberal**<br>1. Increase money supply & decrease interest rates.<br>2. Increase spending & decrease taxes.<br>3. Job creation & price control.<br>4. Tax breaks & subsidies.<br>5. Decrease defense spending. | − | + |
| **Neutral**<br>Combine. | 0 | 0 |
| **SOS or Win-Win**<br>1. Subsidies with strings attached.<br>2. Big subsidies.<br>3. Objective allocation. | ++ | ++ |

## A Simplified Analysis of Inflation and Unemployment

Raising interest rates to decrease inflation may have the effect of decreasing prices by reducing spending from borrowed money. Those benefits may be more than offset by the undesirable effects on reducing the ability of business to borrow for expansion, inventory, and other purposes. The reduction in spending may also have an adverse effect on employment.

Lowering interest rates to decrease unemployment may have little impact because businesses are reluctant to borrow when they are reducing their operations and sales are down. Likewise, consumers are reluctant to borrow when they are already heavily in debt and fearful of a reduction in employment or hours.

Raising taxes and decreasing spending to fight inflation may not be politically feasible. It would also reduce the ability of the government to give tax breaks and well-placed subsidies to increase productivity.

Lowering taxes and increasing spending to fight unemployment may not be politically feasible when the national debt and deficit are already too high.

Increasing the adoption of new technologies and raising the skills of workers to help to reduce inflation by: (1) increasing the productivity of labor to offset increased wages, (2) increasing the quality of goods to offset increased prices, and (3) increasing the GNP and domestic income to further offset increased prices.

Increasing the adoption of new technologies and raising the skills of workers help to reduce unemployment by: (1) making the workers more employable, (2) increasing the GNP and domestic spending to stimulate the creation of more jobs, and (3) increasing the productivity and wage rates thereby offsetting a possible reduction in hours.

The conservative alternative of having interest rates up in times of inflation and down in times of unemployment does not make sense

**Table 3.7   Inflation and Unemployment**

| | GOALS | |
| --- | --- | --- |
| **ALTERNATIVES** | **Conservative** <br> Lower inflation. | **Liberal** <br> Lower unemployment. |
| **Conservative** <br> Change interest rates. | + | − |
| **Liberal** <br> Change taxing and spending. | − | + |
| **Neutral** <br> Little of both. | 0 | 0 |
| **SOS or Win-Win** <br> 1.  Increase new technologies. <br> 2.  Upgrade worker skills. | ++ | ++ |

if inflation and unemployment are problems simultaneously. That would be so if both were over 3 percent. Likewise, the liberal alternative of having a budget surplus in time of inflation and a budget deficit in time of unemployment does not make sense when both inflation and unemployment are over approximately 3 percent. One can, however, stimulate new technologies and upgrade skills when inflation and unemployment are both occurring simultaneously. Also see Table 1.1 and accompanying text.

# Economic Growth

## Economic Growth

Economic growth refers to the annual rate of increase in the gross national product (GNP) or the gross domestic product (GDP). The GNP refers to all income generated in the United States even if it goes to some foreigners. The GDP refers to all income generated anywhere in the world that goes to Americans.

Economic growth is highly important because it provides the increased income that generates increased spending, taxes, jobs, money for government programs, and appropriations for dealing with schools, crimes, health, transportation, communications, food, housing, defense, new technologies, upgrading skills, etc.

**Table 3.8   Economic Growth**

|  | GOALS | |
| --- | --- | --- |
| ALTERNATIVES | Conservative<br>Investment. | Liberal<br>Consumption. |
| **Conservative**<br>Trickle down. | + | − |
| **Liberal**<br>Percolate up. | − | + |
| **Neutral**<br>Both. | 0 | 0 |
| **SOS or Win-Win**<br>Package.  See text. | ++ | ++ |

The conservative approach tends to emphasize taxing and spending that is helpful to investment and business. The increased investment does stimulate economic growth. Conservatives advocate increased investment through lowering taxes on the upper income brackets and lowering the capital gains tax. They also advocate spending for highways, airports, railroads, and other expenditures that will facilitate business profits.

The liberal approach tends to emphasize taxing and spending that is helpful to consumption and workers. The increased consumption does stimulate economic growth. Liberals advocate increased consumption through lowering taxes on the lower income brackets and raising exemptions for dependents and the standard deduction. They also advocate government spending for food stamps, housing vouchers, welfare, teacher salaries, health care, and other government expenditures that result in high consumption.

A SOS package can promote economic growth more directly than through private investment and consumption while still stimulating investment and consumption. Such a package might include the government providing: (1) long-term, large-scale risk capital, (2) a stimulus to competition by readily granting entry permits to all industries and entry of foreign goods into the United States, (3) a stimulus to business and labor to adopt new technologies and upgrade worker skills, (4) funds for relocating workers displaced by tariff reduction, immigration, new technologies, or conversion from defense production, (5) reductions in foreign tariffs to open new markets, (6) immigration policy that brings in innovative, ambitious people with needed skills, (7) free speech to encourage creativity, including suggestions to improve productivity, (8) grants, patents, and purchasing to stimulate inventions but requiring licensing to stimulate diffusion and competition, (9) an educational system that is oriented toward preparation for productive jobs and careers, and (10) conservation of natural resources and a productive, healthful environment.

Other important economic indicators besides economic growth include unemployment, inflation, and measures of income equality. Big economic growth is offset if those other indicators worsen or do not improve. Also see Table 1.2 and accompanying text.

# Chapter 4

---

# Incentives, Growth, and Productivity

This chapter on incentives, growth, and productivity deals with important cross-cutting matters. The idea of increased societal productivity is so important for all the policy problems that it is worth a chapter of its own. Increased resources may be the answer to trade-offs, scarce resources, and deprivation of all kinds. Just as the answer to being poor is to get rich or at least get more money, likewise the answer to how to deal with so many expensive problems is to get more money to deal with them. Getting more money does not mean running printing presses, it means producing goods that have value that can be sold for money.

One might then ask how one increases societal productivity. A key answer is well-placed subsidies and tax breaks. The answer to the question of how one knows a well-placed one from an ill-placed one is that one systematically thinks about the goals, the alternatives, the relations between alternatives and goals, and observes overall scores and sensitivity analysis, as contrasted to a more ideological approach. Saying well-placed subsidies and tax breaks is the same thing as saying providing incentives to be more productive.

## An Incentives Perspective

### Encouraging Socially Desired Behavior in General

All policy problems can be viewed as problems that involve encouraging socially desired behavior. A good checklist for generating ideas on how public policy can encourage socially desired behavior is to think in terms of:

1. Increasing the benefits of doing right.
2. Decreasing the costs of doing right.
3. Increasing the costs of doing wrong.
4. Decreasing the benefits of doing wrong.
5. Increasing the probability that the benefits and costs will occur.

Each specific problem involves different doers, benefits, and costs. For example, an incentives approach to the problems of unemployment and inflation might involve the following five-pronged approach in accordance with the above framework:

1. Tax incentives to business firms and labor unions for keeping prices and wages down. Also monetary incentives to employers to hire the unemployed and monetary incentives to the unemployed to accept training and jobs.
2. Decreasing the costs of finding jobs and workers through better information systems.
3. Increasing the costs of violating price-wage guidelines and work incentives by withdrawing benefits and (in rare cases) fines and other negative penalties.
4. Confiscating the benefits of price-wage violations by special taxes on the gains.
5. More accurate information on prices, wages, and unemployment in order to allocate the benefits and costs more effectively.

As a second example to this kind of perspective, we might look at crime reduction. The following five-pronged approach would be especially appropriate there.

1. The main benefit of complying with the law should be that doing so gives one access to opportunities that are

cut off to law violators. That means legitimate career opportunities must be provided to those who would otherwise turn to crime.

2. One cost of doing right may be a loss of prestige among youthful gang members who consider criminal behavior as an indicator of toughness. There is a need for working to redirect such peer group values so that toughness can be displayed in more constructive ways.

3. The costs of doing wrong can include negative incentives of long prison sentences, but it may be more meaningful to emphasize the withdrawal of career opportunities which would otherwise be present.

4. Provisions should be made for facilitating the confiscation of the property gains of criminal wrongdoing, and decreasing the vulnerability of the targets of crime to lessen the benefits obtained.

5. The probability of arrest and conviction can be increased partly through more professionalism among law enforcement personnel.

One could apply that kind of analysis to all policy problems. One might consider such an approach to be an optimum set of procedures for optimizing societal goals. One can, however, do better than the optimum with regard to procedure as well as substance. Doing better in this context means not having to stimulate people to do the right thing or to deter them from doing the wrong thing. there are two ways to arrange for such situations to never occur— by making them physically or mentally impossible.

An example of making wrongdoing physically impossible is to prohibit sales of cars that can go faster than a certain speed limit, such as 55 miles per hour except in short spurts. Then there is much less need to have a system of punishments for doing wrong or a system designed to determine who the wrongdoers are. Another example would be to prohibit the manufacture of certain kinds of aerosol cans that do great harm to the ozone in the environment. Still another example would be to prohibit the existence of nuclear breeder reactors to supply energy in view of their likelihood of leading to the production of bomb-grade plutonium.

An example of making certain kinds of wrongdoing mentally impossible or close to it is to look at how most people view murder, robbery, burglary, and other street crimes. When affronted in a store, on a bus, or elsewhere, the average person never thinks of pulling a gun or going home and getting one in order to kill the person who has insulted him. Likewise, when driving late at night and observing a convenience store or a gas station that is open with no customers around, the average person never thinks of robbing the place. It is a thought as unthinkable as flapping one's arms to fly to an appointment when one is late. The reason murder and robbery are unthinkable is not that they are physically impossible or because of a fear of the penalties, but because for most people their socialization has been such that those thoughts are not within the realm of normal thinking.

A society operating at the optimum on various policy problems can thus be defined as a society which distributes benefits and costs in such a way as to encourage socially desired behavior with regard to unemployment, inflation, crime, and other social problems, but which also does as much as possible to make the undesirable impossible and/or unthinkable.

## Aspects of Well-Placed Subsidies

A question to address is where the money is going to come from to pay the well-placed subsidies.

1. The usual liberal answer is to take it from defense spending.
2. The usual conservative answer is to take it from domestic spending.
3. The SOS answer is that the subsidy money comes from the subsidy money in the sense that the early subsidies tend to stimulate increased productivity. This generates increased gross national product, which in turn generates increased tax revenues. This

in turn generates a lot more subsidies than were available in the first round, and so on in each subsequent round. It is better than a perpetual motion machine where the output is constant. Here the output keeps increasing.

A question one may raise is whether well-placed subsidies are the answer to all the public policy problems.

1. One answer is that all public policy problems could benefit from well-placed subsidies.
2. Well-placed subsidies alone, however, are not enough for dealing with any of the policy problems.

Examples of other kinds of legislation besides subsidy legislation include:

1. If one wants to improve inner city schools, throwing money at them in the form of compensatory education will not do it because the main drawback to inner city schools is the lack of peer group stimulation toward going on to college. That requires legislation directed toward economic class integration which may mean the use of rent supplements, a different kind of spending than spending for education.
2. On the matter of voter registration and turnout, the key need is legislation which registers people by virtue of the census of on-site registration. That costs no subsidy money. Allowing people to vote in any polling place costs no subsidy money.
3. An example is the Johnson administration's idea of spending $15 billion to eliminate the poverty gap as the solution to the poverty problem.
4. In the context of technological innovation, the need for changing the patent system and the product liability system to facilitate technological innovation and diffusion. This is contrasted with just throwing

money at would-be innovators or would-be adopters.

Every aspect of the poverty problem involves something other than moving every poor person with a family of four from a below $10,000 a year income up to $10,000.

1. On voting rights for the poor, what was said above applies.
2. On educational opportunities, what was said above also applies.
3. On the matter of criminal justice, moving up to the line between poverty and non-poverty is not going to necessarily make a big dent in the extent to which people who are at that line are involved in criminal behavior. It may actually increase their criminal behavior by giving rising expectations. It also is not going to make any significant dent in their ability to hire counsel. A person with a $10,000 income is still going to be dependent on the public defender.
4. Housing opportunities are not going to substantially change. Although they could change, because being at the $10,000 figure rather than the $5,000 figure may put one above a threshold where a rent supplement become more meaningful than living in public housing.
5. Employment opportunities are not going to increase without a program for upgrading skills, though that costs money. But it is different from simply giving a person who has a $5,000 income a negative income tax to bring the person up to $10,000. There is no guarantee that the extra money is going to be spent upgrading skills that will increase employment opportunities.
6. Consumer problems are likely to be just as bad or worse in terms of abusive creditors using abusive collection methods, or in terms of stores in the poorer neighborhoods having poorer quality products that

will not sell in middle class neighborhoods.

## Incentives for Encouraging Socially Desired Behavior

In environmental protection, if public policy wants to encourage socially desired behavior, then one approach to doing so is to make the benefits minus costs of doing right greater than the benefits minus costs of doing wrong.

A second broad approach to encouraging socially desired behavior is to concentrate on building physical and mental blocks against doing wrong, so that potential wrongdoers are not so likely to ever need to think about whether the benefits minus costs of right doing outweigh the benefits minus costs of wrongdoing. One example of a physical block with regard to the pollution (which occurs from people throwing away containers that are not biodegradable) is to simply not have any such containers made. Then public policy does not have to punish people for throwing away the nonexistent containers or reward them for turning them in. Creating biodegradable containers (which largely means paper containers) for products like beer may require a research subsidy to develop the right kind of carton.

An example of a mental block would be to create habits of throwing things in wastebaskets on the part of children to the point where it becomes unthinkable that as adults they would push an old refrigerator or a car into a river, rather than bring it to a junkyard. They bring it to the junkyard not because they are worried about being fined, but because the behavior of putting such non-biodegradable metal into blocking a river is unthinkable for a civilized human being.

## Necessity-Invention

Saving that necessity-invention will take care of it is not enough. The time span may be way too long. Necessity-invention will eventually work, but a lot of harm will be done if the process is not accelerated. Necessity-invention may result in only a minimally satisfactory invention. It does not guarantee anything highly imaginative or highly useful or highly SOS. It simply guarantees meeting a minimum threshold. It simply means finding an oil substitute. The oil substitute may be very expensive, very inefficient, but a substitute.

In order to stimulate faster and better necessity-invention, the well-placed subsidies are needed. In the case of battery development, Japan is working on the problem with well-placed subsidies. There is nothing in the way of any kind of big program in the United States, nothing approaching a man on the moon, or the Manhattan Project, or a cure for cancer. The need for an electric substitute for oil, though, may be as great as those. Some may be much greater than finding a way to get a man on the moon.

## A Growth Perspective

In discussing the general means for achieving the super-optimum goals, one must recognize that those means are going to cost large amounts of money for appropriate subsidies, tax breaks, and some forms of regulation. A super-optimum perspective tends to be optimistic in setting goals and in believing that the means can be found for achieving them. This is not, however, a naively optimistic approach, but rather one that is based on what is realistically possible, especially if one proceeds with a positive orientation.

A growth perspective implies that the funding to support the achievement of the super-optimum goals will come mainly from growth of the economy rather than from a redistribution of wealth. In fact, a redistribution from the rich to the poor may interfere with economic growth by unduly reducing incentives to save, invest, and even work as hard or as well as one otherwise would, regardless whether one is rich or poor. Likewise, a redistribution from the poor to the rich through regressive taxes and investment incentives could also similarly interfere with economic growth and public morale.

A growth perspective tends to be endorsed by both conservatives (who favor supply-side economics) and by liberals (who favor industrial policy and economic planning). They even tend to agree that the main means to economic growth are tax breaks and subsidies, although they may disagree as to exactly what form they should take.

Some of the costs could be covered by improving the U.S. defense capability at a lower cost by concentrating more on weapons systems which are more effective and efficient. That may mean more emphasis on Trident submarines and low-flying cruise missiles, and less emphasis on easily destroyed B-1 bombers, aircraft carriers, and MX missile silos. It may also mean more realistic defense systems, such as a radar and laser-firing system for destroying enemy nuclear submarines, rather than a star wars system for supposedly destroying all incoming enemy missiles. Making defense expenditures more effective and efficient and thereby reducing them makes more sense. This is in contrast to increasing questionable defense expenditures by taking from on-the-job training programs and subsidies for technological innovation. It is no coincidence that the United States and Russia had been ranking lowest among the industrial nations on productivity growth since about 1980, and highest among the industrial nations on defense expenditures.

On the matter of bipartisan growth, both conservatives and liberals also tend to endorse the idea of more systematic governmental decision-making in order to achieve economic growth. Conservatives consider such decision-making to be a form of bringing good business practice to government. Liberals consider it to be a form of economic planning. Systematic governmental decision-making manifests itself in using contemporary methods of benefit-cost analysis to: (1) choose among discrete alternatives, (2) choose under conditions of risk, (3) choose where doing too much or too little is undesirable, and (4) to allocate scarce resources in light of given goals and relations.

## Incentives Related to Growth

With regard to the relationship between incentives and productivity, we have a set of ideas including:

1. The retooling of industries that are using relatively obsolete capital.
2. The employing of people who are relatively unproductive or underproductive. That has two sides to it. One side is the incentives needed to get the employers to do the employing. The other side is the incentives to get the potential employees to move, to get into training programs, to accept the jobs offered, and to show up for work.
3. If productivity is a function of capital, labor, and natural resources, we should say something about natural resources although we do not have to have symmetry or equality on all three dimensions. There does not seem to be anything that is seriously wrong with out natural resources, as contrasted to our capital and labor. Natural resources mainly means land, minerals, and energy resources. We have great land. It could be taken better care of with better conservation and irrigation, but there is ot a serious problem in American productivity. We have no great shortage on minerals.

It is the energy part of the land-mineral-energy sub-breakdown of natural resources on which we are doing poorly. The American energy picture is close to miserable. In central Illinois, a good deal of potential economic development is not possible because the wasteful Clinton nuclear-energy plant now makes energy costs too high for business firms that would otherwise locate in the area. This is happening in many places in the United States. The costs of energy are becoming too high to locate in various areas that otherwise would be good places. There is also the sin of omission relating to the failure to take advantage of energy sources that could be inexpensively developed, including modern nuclear energy and modern solar energy. Perhaps Washington will eventually push for a new nuclear energy program that provides cost-effective and safe energy. Doing so would involve modern techniques that the private energy industry in the United States has refused to adopt. The reasons are partly their inertia in getting into costly and unsafe techniques, and then lacing incentives to get out of them since they have monopolistic customer relations. Electricity may be the most incompetent, inefficient major industry in the United States. Unfortunately it is quite basic since all industry depends on energy to run factories, regardless what the factories are making.

Recent world developments affect the defense capability factor. The idea of meaningful arms control is now more a possibility than it has been. The seriousness of the trade and budget deficits has, however, become greater. The idea of increasing productivity by putting relatively unproductive people to work previously referred to people in the labor force who were unemployed. The idea has now expanded to include the aged, the handicapped, preschool mothers, the underemployed, and the unsatisfactorily employed. They were either generally not counted as being in the labor force, or were wrongly counted as being employed. For our purposes a person is not employed or at least is not fully employed if they are not working in accordance with their productive abilities.

Incentives and productivity are the means and national well-being is the end. There is a reciprocal relationship in the sense that incentives stimulate productivity, which stimulates national well-being, which in turn stimulates incentives money. Although lowering the trade and budget deficits are goals, the really important goal is economic growth. Those two deficits are just side effects. It is fine that they get reduced, but what we are primarily concerned with is national prosperity at an increasing rate and widespread across regions, rural and urban areas, rich and poor, black and white, male and female, and other societal groups.

# Productivity

## Japanese and American Productivity

The typical Japanese firm wants to be the most important firm in the industry even if it is losing money. The typical American firm is happy with being 20th in the industry if it is making profits.

The big indicator should be which of those two basic orientations is better for society and the global market. The Japanese approach is much better if becoming first in the industry is achieved by making high quality products at low prices, even if the firm almost goes bankrupt doing so. The world benefits even if the firm loses. The American firm that is making big profits and providing the work with low quality merchandise at high prices is obviously less socially desirable.

Japanese firms are sometimes killing themselves out of a desire to be on top. But not to be on top by using cheap-shot advertising with sexy girls on American cars which just appeals to people's worst instinct in getting them to buy products.

Both the American firms and the Japanese firms are operating to promote their own self-interests. The difference is that the Japanese concept of self-interest is to be acclaimed as the leader in the field. The American concept is just to make a lot of money even if the products are disliked, as long as you can sell them for more than they cost to make. American products are not necessarily disliked, but they are sometimes laughed at like gas guzzlers in developing countries.

Even on research and development, American firms do not deserve so much credit. Most American R & D is developed in American universities, not American business firms. The United States deserves a lot of credit for inventiveness, including the winning of Nobel prizes, but that is not General Motors. That is the University of Illinois and other universities. Japan does poorly on that score in both its business firms and its universities. They are not cash contributors to the world when it comes to inventiveness. They are implementers, rather than inventors.

Each business firm in the world trying to maximize income minus expenses is by no means good for the world, rather than maximizing market share. This does more to refute Adam Smith and traditional capitalism than anything Karl Marx had to say. Marx was operating largely out of theory, rather than out of the experience that had not yet arrived in the world.

The Japanese business firms are doing well in that they are moving toward 100% of the market share in many basic industries of the world. They will probably never reach the point of 100 percent, but that is what they are striving for. Yet they or their companies are not getting rich, in terms of income over expenses and assets over liabilities. The reasons are:

1.  They charge low prices that hurt how much profit they can make on a Toyota or Sony TV set because they want to sell a lot of Toyotas. They want as high a percent of the market as possible.
2.  They provide all kinds of benefits to the consumer that are expensive to the manufacturer but that help sell their products and thereby increase their market share.
3.  They deviate substantially from what is taught in American business schools. They are lowering their revenue by lowering their prices. They are increasing their expenses by offering various features that no regulatory agency is requiring them to offer.
4.  Yet they are greatly disrupting the business of U.S. Steel, General Motors, and other giants of American industry. Japan is benefitting because this practice means lots of income for Japanese workers and lots of income in the form of taxes for Japanese government. The Japanese CEOs are not exactly impoverished, but they do no live as luxuriously as the people who run General Motors and U.S. Steel who are doing a poorer job.

Competition is fine for the quality of life of the world and a nation that competes well like Japan does. That, however, is not advertising competition. It is also not cheating competition where a business firm sees how much it can cheat its customers or cheat its workers. It is competition to see who can produce the most sought-after product because of its low price and its quality content. That may be crazy behavior, but Japan as a nation is laughing hysterically all the way to the bank.

**Increased Productivity as an Upward Spiral**

That is a new kind of indirect effect that is part of an upward spiral idea as contrasted to a vicious circle or downward spiral idea. The previous aspects include:

Multiplier effect whereby increased productivity means increased income to whoever is being more productive. That person's increased income means increased spending, which means increased income for others, and so on down a multiplier line. The multiplier effect is an example of increased productivity producing further increased productivity, because the income earned becomes someone else's income by way of spending. Some of that may go into savings which is available for investment purposes and thereby means increased productivity. Even the portion that goes into consumption may stimulate increased productivity by firms that are seeking to capture that consumption money.

The compounding effect whereby increased productivity means increased income to whoever is being more productive. That means the person who is paying more in taxes is given a constant or even slightly decreasing tax rate. If that tax money gets into well-placed subsidies to produce more productivity, then in that sense the increased productivity is being compounded. Society is getting interest on its interest, or growth on its growth.

The intergenerational effect whereby the increased productivity of an adult serves as an inspirational role model for a child or grandchild, thereby increasing the child's productivity.

The fourth aspect of the upward spiral is increased productivity that may manifest itself in new products that consumers want to have such as cars, televisions, video players, etc. The existence of those products causes people to be more productive so they can earn more income in order to buy them. In the absence of those products, people have less incentive to work harder since those products which they desire to not exist.

## Council on International Competitiveness

Management wants low wages, workers want high wages; the government takes a hands-off position until a compromise is reached. Two years later maybe the company is out of business because it has shortsightedly failed to keep up with international competition. That is a super lose-lose situation where management gave in to some extent on low wages, workers gave in to some extent on high wages, and management goes bankrupt and workers are out of a job because they were too shortsighted to see what the real needs of both sides are. That is the essence of the Japanese success story, namely the government (or more specifically the Ministry of International Trade and Investment) providing the foresightedness that neither management nor labor can admittedly provide so well. Workers want higher wages now, not the possibility of bigger income later. Management wants to cut expenses now, not the possibility of higher profits later. This is a super-maximum solution in which everybody suffers including management, labor, and especially society.

It is partly a matter of semantics. If one talks about the government, that creates a negative intervention of some kind of regulatory agency. If one talks about Ministry of International Trade and Investment (MITI), that may create some kind of images of Japanese intervention, at least with regard to ideas. Americans find it hard to believe that somebody else, even Japan, may have developed a better way of running an economy. There is a need for an American phrase like MITI. We already have it, although it is currently of questionable value, namely the Council on Competitiveness. Its custom has been to argue in favor of lower wages, longer hours without overtime, unsafe workplaces, cutting environmental standards, cutting on union involvement, and cutting on everything.

The Council's position is that our international competitiveness is increased by cutting expenses and thereby enabling business firms to be able to lower their prices. Big fallacies in that include:

1. Cutting expenses results in fatter profits, not lower prices.
2. The cutting of labor costs is a disincentive to auto-

mate. Anything that is a disincentive to automate is a real evil with regard to increasing international competitiveness.

3. The whole philosophy of cutting expenses and raising prices is what had gotten the United States into trouble internationally in losing customers to the Japanese philosophy of increasing market share by providing more expensive quality and lowering prices.

4. Always taking the management side against society and against the workers destroys the credibility of the Council. It does not have the image of being above partisan battles, like the MITI has.

# Chapter 5

# Organizing the Economy

## Philosophical Background

### The Marxist Dialectic

Capitalism in this context means private ownership and operation of the major means of production and distribution. Socialism means government ownership and operation of the major means of production and distribution. A mixed economy means some private ownership/operation and some government ownership/operation.

Ideal communism in the Marxist sense means each according to his ability and each according to his needs, rather than according to his output. That is a more equitable system. It is unclear though as to

**Table 5.1   Marxist Dialectic**

| | GOALS | |
| --- | --- | --- |
| ALTERNATIVES | Conservative<br>Productivity. | Liberal<br>Equity. |
| Conservative<br>Capitalism. | + | − |
| Liberal<br>Socialism. | − | + |
| Neutral<br>Mixed economy. | 0 | 0 |
| SOS or Win-Win<br>Ideal communism. | ++ | ++ |

how it is a more productive system. It does involve a lower tax burden if there is going to be a withering away of the state.

Ideal communism is a SOS alternative only in terms of the perceptions of Karl Marx, not necessarily in terms of the realities of how communism has developed in the twentieth century. There has been no indication of movement toward a withering away of the state, distribution solely in accordance with needs, or increased productivity without government and without monetary incentives.

## Disputes between Ideologies

Later in this chapter we talk about competition as a variable that distinguishes socialism versus capitalism. That discussion is less philosophical than talking about socialism and capitalism ideologies. Ideologies talk in terms of freedom and symbolism as goals, rather than the more mundane goals of higher profits and lower prices.

**Table 5.2　Ideologies**

| | GOALS | |
| --- | --- | --- |
| **ALTERNATIVES** | **Conservative**<br>1. Entrepreneurial freedom.<br>2. Capitalistic symbolism. | **Liberal**<br>1. Political freedom.<br>2. Socialistic symbolism. |
| **Conservative**<br>Private ownership. | + | − |
| **Liberal**<br>Government ownership. | − | + |
| **Neutral**<br>Regulated private ownership and mixed economy. | 0 | 0 |
| **SOS or Win-Win**<br>1. Competitive economy.<br>2. Competitive political system. | ++ | ++ |

Table 5.2 is also more broadly concerned with having both a competitive economy and a competitive political system, and not just economic competition.

# Socialism versus Capitalism

## A SOS Solution to Socialistic versus Capitalistic Farm Ownership

Productive farms and property refer to producing a lot of goods at low cost. Equitable farms and property mainly refers to no exploitation of labor, no despoiling of the environment, and no excessive holdings.

The above table deals only with ownership of farmland. Later in this chapter, we discuss a broader analysis of government versus private ownership and operation in the context of factories (as well as farmland) and possibly public schools, post offices, and municipal transportation.

**Table 5.3    Socialistic versus Capitalistic Farm Ownership**

| | GOALS | |
|---|---|---|
| **ALTERNATIVES** | **Conservative** Productive farms and property. | **Liberal** Equitable farms and property. |
| **Conservative** Land to the highest bidder. | + | − |
| **Liberal** Retain collective farming. | − | + |
| **Neutral** Collective farming with private plots. | 0 | 0 |
| **SOS or Win-Win** Government ownership with contracting out to farming farmers. | ++ | ++ |

## Alternative Ways of Relating the Government to the Economy

Socialism refers to government ownership and public policy designed to facilitate equality of income and wealth. Capitalism refers to private ownership with no public policy designed to facilitate equality of income and wealth.

Table 5.4 below indicates that the policy which is best depends greatly on the relative weight assigned the goals. One could conceivably talk in terms of four policies: (1) private ownership and no equality, (2) private ownership and equality, (3) government ownership and no equality, and (4) government ownership and equality. The two elements of capitalism do tend to go together, as do the two elements of socialism.

One can have democratic or dictatorial capitalism and democratic or dictatorial socialism, depending on whether there are universal voting rights and minority political rights.

**Table 5.4    (Old) Government to the Economy**

| | GOALS | |
| --- | --- | --- |
| | **Conservative**<br>1. More opportunity to go further.<br>2. More initiative to take changes.<br>3. More enterprise freedom and consumer sovereignty. | **Liberal**<br>1. Equality of opportunity.<br>2. More security.<br>3. More political freedom and popular control. |
| **ALTERNATIVES** | | |
| **Conservative**<br>Capitalism. | + | − |
| **Liberal**<br>Socialism. | − | + |
| **Neutral**<br>Mixed economy. | 0 | 0 |
| **SOS or Win-Win**<br>See text. | ++ | ++ |

One can have responsive or non-responsive capitalism and responsive or non-responsive socialism. Responsiveness in this context refers to being responsive to consumers and workers. Socialism is traditionally thought of as being more responsive to consumers and workers. If one weights responsiveness heavily, then responsive capitalism and responsive socialism would be undesirable. Table 5.4 may, however, be helpful in deciding between responsive capitalism and responsive socialism.

## A SOS Evaluation of Capitalism versus Socialism

The two most important goals here may be the conservative concern for business profits and the liberal concern for low prices to consumers.

In tables 5.4 and 5.5, the SOS alternative emphasizes having a competitive economy. That can be brought about through subsidizing the startup costs of competing firms, rather than resorting to anti-trust regulation or other forms of regulation.

**Table 5.5    Capitalism versus Socialism**

| | GOALS | |
|---|---|---|
| **ALTERNATIVES** | **Conservative**<br>Profits and GNP. | **Liberal**<br>Creativity. |
| **Conservative**<br>Unregulated private<br>ownership. | + | − |
| **Liberal**<br>Monopolistic government<br>ownership. | − | + |
| **Neutral**<br>Mixed economy. | 0 | 0 |
| **SOS or Win-Win**<br>Competitive economy. | ++ | ++ |

**Government versus Private Ownership and Operation**

The SOS alternative of contracting out to private operations can be applied to public schools, post offices, and municipal transportation. In former socialistic countries, it can apply also to contracting out government-owned factories and land.

The contracting out does not have to be to only one private entrepreneur. The two most qualified lowest bidders can both receive contracts for different geographical areas, sectors of the industry, or other aspects of the contract in order to encourage competition.

Productivity and the liberal goals can be further increased through appropriate government incentives by way of well-placed tax credits and subsidies. That goes beyond what can be achieved by way of government ownership or control combined with contracting out to private operation.

**Table 5.6   Ownership and Operation**

|  | GOALS | |
| --- | --- | --- |
|  | **Conservative**<br>High productivity. | **Liberal**<br>1. Equity.<br>2. Workplace quality.<br>3. Environmental<br>    protection. |
| **ALTERNATIVES** |  | 4. Consumer protection. |
| **Conservative**<br>Private ownership and<br>operation (capitalism). | + | − |
| **Liberal**<br>Government ownership<br>and operation (socialism). | − | + |
| **Neutral**<br>Some government and<br>some private. | 0 | 0 |
| **SOS or Win-Win**<br>1. 100% government<br>    owned.<br>2. 100% private<br>    operation. | ++ | ++ |

**Table 5.7 (Simple) Ownership and Operation**

| | GOALS | |
| | Conservative | Liberal |
| ALTERNATIVES | High productivity. | Equity. |
| --- | --- | --- |
| **Conservative** Government ownership and operation (socialism). | + | – |
| **Liberal** (Private ownership and operation (capitalism). | – | + |
| **Neutral** Some government and some private. | 0 | 0 |
| **SOS or Win-Win** 1. 100% government owned and 100% private operation. 2. 100% private with government incentives. | ++ | ++ |

Table 5.7 is a simplified version of Table 5.6. The four liberal goals can be considered as having been combined under the one liberal goal of equity, or they can be considered as having been dropped as being less important than equity. In Table 5.6 the liberal goals are equity, workplace quality, environmental protection, and consumer protection. In Table 5.7, the liberal goals have been reduced to equity.

Table 5.6 partly seeks to emphasize that workplace quality, environmental protection, and consumer protection are not necessarily promoted by government ownership. The socialist steel mills in Poland were a good example of poor workplace quality under socialism. The socialistic TVA in the United States was a good example of poor environmental protection under socialism. Government-owned power companies having monopoly control are good examples of the lack of consumer protection under socialism.

All of these goals can be better achieved by requiring them as part of a contract. That is likely to produce greater compliance than traditional government regulation. The threat of not having the contract renewed but instead having it go to a competing company can generate greater compliance. That is better than relying on the supposed altruism of managers of government factories who are not rewarded or punished for complying with goals.

Table 5.7 also emphasizes that the government can provide further incentives by way of well-placed subsidies and tax credits to supplement the liberal contract provisions.

# Competition as a Key Factor

### Competition as a SOS Economic Solution

The conservative alternative of an unregulated marketplace may lead to only one or a few firms dominating most industries. That arrangement may be profitable in the short run, although contrary to low prices.

The liberal alternative of government ownership or tight regulation tends to mean a government monopoly or stifled private enterprise. That means reduced business profits, although it might mean artificially low prices to satisfy consumers as voters.

The mixed economy scores in the middle on both business profits and low prices.

The SOS alternative may draw upon the stimulus to innovation and efficiency of private profit-making. The SOS alternative may encourage competition through well-placed seed money. Doing so results in lower prices through a competitive marketplace, rather than through a monopolistic one or through artificial price constraints.

The marketplace is associated with capitalism. It may not be associated with competition if the marketplace leads to monopolies or firms working together to decrease competition.

Regulation or government ownership is associated with socialism. It is even more likely to lead to monopoly, but monopoly in the hands of the state rather than private enterprise.

The marketplace may lead to better business profits than regulation does. Regulation may lead to better consumer prices than the marketplace does.

**Table 5.8   Competition**

| | GOALS | |
|---|---|---|
| **ALTERNATIVES** | **Conservative** Business profits. | **Liberal** Consumer prices. |
| **Conservative** Marketplace (capitalism). | + | – |
| **Liberal** Regulation (socialism). | – | + |
| **Neutral** Some of each. | 0 | 0 |
| **SOS or Win-Win** Competition. | ++ | ++ |

## Competition in the Public and Private Sectors

The purpose of this section is to discuss ideas relating to such matters in the private sector as: (1) competition and cooperation occurring simultaneously, (2) competition versus monopoly, (3) encouraging competition and cooperation in the workplace, marketplace, academia, and the world, and (4) innovative ideas about competition. Ideas discussed relevant to the public sector include consolidation versus competition among agencies and competition within public schools, police departments, and political parties.

Both competition and cooperation occur simultaneously in a workplace where workers work as a team for their workplace unit or their firm. At the same time, the firm is highly competitive with other firms. Good examples are found in sports such as basketball. The players have to cooperate in order for the team to win, but the team may be highly competitive in dealing with other teams. Both cooperation and competition are approved in that kind of workplace context.

Competition is usually, however, more likely to be contrasted with monopoly or oligopoly, when we are talking about the economy as a whole. Competition among business firms is good for consumers in bringing prices down and quality up in order to attract consumers.

It is good for workers to have business firms compete for their services. Competition may be good for businesses, especially if it makes entry into new markets possible. Competition also provides business with an incentive to do better and become more profitable. Competition also encourages the firms to be watchdogs over each other regarding possible bribery or other law violations. Monopoly, on the other hand, is bad for consumers, workers, potentially competing businesses, and society in general.

There are various ways of encouraging competition. Some examples are: (1) anti-trust laws, (2) funding startup companies with seed money, (3) abolishing tariffs, (4) requiring electricity and phone companies to rent their infrastructures, (5) giving inventors exclusive access to royalties, but not monopolistic manufacturing, and (6) encouraging mergers that lead countervailing power.

On a broader level, society can encourage a competitive spirit through childhood socialization. This involves encouraging children to do well wherever their abilities and interests lie for which there is a demand. Such socialization should also emphasize the importance of improving one's competitive success through collaboration. It should also de-emphasize the stigma associated with seeking to destroy competitors, rather than outdo them.

Public administration has traditionally frowned on government agencies overlapping or competing with each other. That tradition may be undesirable for getting things done. For example, if finding jobs for displaced workers is a highly important policy problem, then it should be pursued at the national, provincial, and local levels. Likewise, if environmental protection is highly important then it should be pursued by legislatures, courts, and multiple executive agencies such as departments of agriculture, commerce, labor, interior, justice, and state.

Competition may be especially important within public schools, police departments, and political parties. Both teachers and police can be paid on a merit basis, both as individuals and as members of units. Statistics can be frequently published comparing classrooms, schools, police stations, police departments, and other units, although taking care to make sure that the statistics are reasonably accurate.

Competition can be encouraged among political parties with such means as: (1) creating geographical districts that are equal in population but with lines drawn so as to make the political parties as equal as possible within districts, (2) making it relatively easy for third parties and minor parties to get on the ballot, (3) requiring primary elections to choose candidates thereby providing more competition within the political parties, and (4) requiring chief executives to be bipartisan in appointing judges, commissioners, and other members of multi-member boards.

## Equality as a Key Factor in Socialism and Capitalism

Capitalism differs from socialism mainly in terms of government versus private ownership and operation of the major means of production and distribution. Capitalism also differs from socialism with regard to the extent to which inequality of income and wealth is allowed.

Under pure capitalism, there are no limits to the degree of permissible inequality in income and wealth. Under socialism, there are progressive income taxes and inheritance taxes designed to promote a substantial amount of equality in income and wealth.

Capitalism justifies economic inequality as a stimulus to increased productivity. The theory is people will work harder and be more innovative in order to receive the rewards of greater income and wealth.

Socialism justifies having greater income equality as the fair or equitable thing to do, especially in the context of providing a minimum floor regarding food, shelter, and clothing to the poor.

A SOS alternative that does well on both the conservative and liberal goals involves allowing considerable inequality in income and wealth but providing a minimum floor. That can be done through a negative income tax whereby people who are below the minimum level receive a payment from the Internal Revenue Service instead of paying taxes.

A better approach is to emphasize the earned income credit whereby the people below a minimum level who work are rewarded by receiving an IRS payment. Those who do not work receive public aid and assistance in finding a job. The SOS may also provide tax breaks and subsidies for upgrading individual skills in order to increase one's productivity.

## Equality, Equal Opportunity, and Merit Treatment

All people are not created equal, but they should be given equal opportunity to be creative. Doing that, however, might require equalizing people genetically and socially to provide equal opportunities. Maybe the correct concept is equal treatment under law as expressed by the U.S. Constitution and the U.S. Supreme Court.

Perhaps what is really important is merit treatment, with a floor below which no one is allowed to fall. Merit treatment means that inequalities above that floor are based as much as possible on one's interests, abilities, motivation, prior output, future potential, and other merit considerations. In this context, merit treatment means relevant to job performance. Thus in an ideal society, pay and other rewards would be based on such merit considerations as much as possible.

Merit rewards encourage creativity. It is difficult to be creative if one is not rewarded for being creative. On the other hand, some argue that some discrimination encourages creativity to offset the discrimination. Such an argument might apply to moderate economic discrimination. That means not everyone has the same income or wealth. Moderate differentials can be an incentive to both the poor and the rich to get richer so long as the poor (especially children) are never allowed to fall below a minimum level on health, education, and necessities broadly defined. Even non-merit discrimination based on gender or ethnic affiliation is more demoralizing than inspirational.

Regardless of the pragmatic effects of merit treatment, it can be considered desirable as good in itself or in accordance with the golden rule of virtually all religions and ethical systems. The golden rule says, "Do unto others as you would have others do unto you." This emphasizes interaction between individuals. Merit treatment tends to emphasize interaction between ethnic groups, genders, and other demographic groups.

Merit treatment can also be extended to interaction among nations, which is the basis of free trade and the theory of comparative advantage. One can even say that the only major point on which Adam Smith and Karl Marx both agreed is the basic principle of specialization and division of labor. That principle says people, groups, and nations should be encouraged to do whatever they can do best in terms of their abilities and interests for which there is a demand.

Thus merit treatment is a high-level win-win principle. It is on a level along with the win-win importance of economic competition, lifetime education, new technologies, democracy, and peaceful dispute resolution.

1. Merit treatment is relevant to developmental policy studies, which is concerned with inequality between industrial countries and developing countries. Merit treatment is also essential or highly helpful to national economic development.

2. The item is also relevant to policy evaluation because a key policy problem in any country is how to deal with the privileges of the rich versus the deprivations of the poor, and how to facilitate people operating at their best.

3. The item is further relevant to creativity  because discrimination discourages creativity, and merit treatment encourages it, especially along gender, ethnic, class, and other lines.

# Section B

# Improving the
# Factors of Production

# Chapter 6

# Land and Agriculture

## The U.S. Farm Income Problem

### Evaluating Policies for Dealing with the Farm Income Problem

The conservative alternative would win on the conservative total if more weight were given to farmer income. The importance of farmer income has been lessening even among conservatives along with the lessening of political power of farmers.

Table 6.1    Farm Income

| | GOALS | |
|---|---|---|
| | **Conservative**<br>Increase farmer<br>income. | **Liberal**<br>1. Increase consumer<br>benefits. |
| **ALTERNATIVES** | | 2. Equity. |
| **Conservative**<br>1. Decrease supply.<br>2. Increase government demand. | + | − |
| **Liberal**<br>1. Increase consumer demand.<br>2. Increase direct payments.<br>3. Less farmers.<br>4. Decrease farm expense. | − | + |
| **Neutral**<br>All. | 0 | 0 |
| **SOS or Win-Win**<br>World marketplace with $<br>deficit down. | ++ | ++ |

American farmers are potentially capable of competing well in the world marketplace given their efficient technology, land, and agricultural methods. The value of the dollar since 1980 has been relatively high due to government borrowing to meet the national debt. This has interfered with other countries being able to get dollars to buy American farm products as easily in comparison to obtaining the kind of money needed to buy farm products from Canada, Australia, Argentina, or elsewhere.

## Negotiating Free Trade in Farm Products

Table 6.2 is based on a September 1993 news report that the United States is seeking to have France reduce its subsidies to French soybean farmers. A $1 subsidy can have the same effect as a $1 tariff. In the case of a $1 tariff, a $2 quantity of U.S. soybeans costs the French consumer $3, which is higher than the $2.50 that the French farmer charges. In the case of the $1 subsidy, the French farmer can make a profit by charging $1.50, which undercuts the $2 charged by the American farmer.

**Table 6.2          Free Trade in Farm Products**

| | GOALS | |
|---|---|---|
| **ALTERNATIVES** | **Conservative** Aid U.S. producers (raise profits). | **Liberal** Aid U.S. consumers (lower prices). |
| **Conservative** Retaliatory tariff increases (increase 20%). | + | − |
| **Liberal** Lower U.S. tariffs without return (decrease 20%). | − | + |
| **Neutral** Keep tariffs as they are. | 0 | 0 |
| **SOS or Win-Win** Reciprocal tariff reduction. | ++ | ++ |

The conservative U.S. negotiator threatens a big tariff increase on French wines to force the soybean subsidy down. That may help American wine producers, but it hurts American wine consumers.

The liberal U.S. negotiator may lower U.S. wine tariffs without receiving much in return. That hurts U.S. wine producers, but it helps American wine consumers.

The SOS may be to agree to lower the U.S. tariff on French wines if France will lower the subsidy on French soybeans. The result is that U.S. soybean producers, U.S. wine consumers, and French soybean consumers are all helped.

That reciprocal arrangement is a net plus to the United States if we have more soybean producers than wine producers, and if the U.S. wine producers can be diverted into something more profitable. The arrangement is also a net plus to France if they have more wine producers than soybean producers, and the French soybean producers can be diverted into something more profitable.

This kind of mutually beneficial reciprocal tariff reduction is a good example of a SOS where all sides come out ahead. This can be contrasted to a neutral compromise between a retaliatory increase and a unilateral decrease. Such a compromise of retaining the tariffs may hurt U.S. soybean producers, U.S. wine consumers, French wine producers, and French soybean consumers. The harm is greater than a reciprocal reduction, although not so bad as a retaliatory tariff increase on French wine, which may even increase French farm subsidies, rather than reduce them.

## Agriculture and Developing Nations

### Pricing Food in China and Elsewhere

In China and other developing nations, farmers want high prices for their food products or else they threaten to switch to coffee or drugs or other non-food products. Urban workers want low prices as food consumers. The government often tends to side with the urban workers which may create food shortages in Africa and elsewhere.

The SOS of a price supplement involves farmers receiving 101 percent of the price they are asking, but urban workers and others paying only 79 percent which is less than the 80 percent that they are willing and able to pay.

The difference of 22 percent is made up by food stamps given to the urban workers in return for agreeing to be in programs that upgrade their skills and productivity. The food stamps are used to pay for staple products (like rice or wheat) along with cash. Farmers can then redeem the stamps for cash, provided that they also agree to be in programs that increase their productivity.

Food stamps have administrative feasibility for ease in determining that workers and farmers are doing what they are supposed to do in return for the food stamps. They cannot be easily counterfeited. They serve as a check on how much the farmers have sold.

By increasing the productivity of farmers and workers, the secondary effects occur of improving farming methods, increasing exports, increasing the importing of new technologies, and increasing the GNP.

High prices are not politically feasible because of too much opposition from workers who consume but do not produce food. The high prices though are acceptable if they can be met by way of price supplements in the form of food stamps.

**Table 6.3     Pricing Food**

|  | GOALS | |
|---|---|---|
| **ALTERNATIVES** | **Conservative**<br>Rural well being. | **Liberal**<br>Urban well being. |
| **Conservative**<br>High price. | + | − |
| **Liberal**<br>Low price. | − | + |
| **Neutral**<br>Compromise. | 0 | 0 |
| **SOS or Win-Win**<br>Price supplement. | ++ | ++ |

## Food Pricing and Developing Nations

Table 6.4 is a simplified version of Table 6.3. It emphasizes the conservative goal of the well being of people in the farming business and the liberal goal of the well being of consumers of food products. The notes to the previous table are also applicable here.

In both tables, the SOS alternative is for the consumers to pay a relatively low price and the farmers to receive a relatively high price. This comes by way of vouchers or price supplements that are given to the consumers which can be redeemed by the farmers. Both the consumer-workers and the farmers could be expected to participate in programs designed to improve their productivity in return for these price supplements.

## Land Reform in Developing Countries

If we are talking about 100 units of land, the conservative alternative is to retain those 100 units in a single owner. The liberal alternative is to divide all 100 units among approximately ten families or some other quantity. The compromise would be divide half the land and let the original owner retain the other half.

**Table 6.4      (Simple) Food Pricing**

| | GOALS | |
|---|---|---|
| **ALTERNATIVES** | **Conservative** Rural well being. | **Liberal** Urban well being. |
| **Conservative** High price. 60. | + | – |
| **Liberal** Low price. 40. | – | + |
| **Neutral** Middle price. 50. | 0 | 0 |
| **SOS or Win-Win** 1. 61 to firms. 2. 49 to workers (with food stamps). | ++ | ++ |

**Table 6.5    Land Reform**

|  | GOALS | |
| ALTERNATIVES | Conservative<br>Productivity. | Liberal<br>Equity. |
| --- | --- | --- |
| **Conservative**<br>Retain land (0 units). | + | – |
| **Liberal**<br>Divide land (100 units). | – | + |
| **Neutral**<br>Compromise (50 units). | 0 | 0 |
| **SOS or Win-Win**<br>1. Buy the land.<br>2. Lots of land.<br>3. Co-op action. | ++ | ++ |

The conservative goal emphasizes the productivity of large landholdings, especially with modern farm machinery. The liberal goal emphasizes the equity or fairness of sharing land or other natural resources.

The SOS alternative (whereby all sides can come out ahead of their best initial expectations) involves: (1) buying the land at good prices by the government for distribution, (2) encouraging cooperative use of modern machinery among the ten or so farm families, and (3) encouraging participation in programs designed to upgrade the skills of farm workers so they can make more income in non-farm activities in view of the lessening need for farm workers with modern technology.

Some of the funding for buying the land for redistribution purposes can come from the World Bank, the International Monetary Fund, and industrialized nations like the United States. That kind of outside funding is a good investment especially if it decreases the likelihood of warfare between landless peasants and land owners. Promoting peace and prosperity in developing countries (partly through land reform) can facilitate those countries being better customers, suppliers, and outlets for investment to the more industrialized countries.

# Government Owned Land

The traditional conservative policy on federal lands is to allow a maximum of commercial use. The traditional liberal policy is to allow a minimum of commercial use or none at all.

The compromise position is to allow for multiple uses. That means such commercial uses as grazing, mining, farming, or oil development. It also means such non-commercial uses as wilderness and recreation.

Conservatives are interested in profits and adding to the GNP. Liberals are oriented toward a goal of preservation for nature or use by the general public.

A SOS alternative might involve contracting out certain portions, but with rules that specify the land must be restored and it must not be abused while it is being used. The contract would be in the form of a lease with the high rents going to promoting environmental protection. The government can also receive a royalty on minerals or other things of value that are taken from the land. Such a solution could be profitable and income producing. It could also provide for accompanying non-commercial development and preservation.

**Table 6.6   Federal Lands**

| | GOALS | |
| --- | --- | --- |
| **ALTERNATIVES** | **Conservative**<br>1. Increase profits.<br>2. Increase GNP. | **Liberal**<br>Preservation. |
| **Conservative**<br>Allow commercial use. | + | − |
| **Liberal**<br>Prohibit commercial use. | − | + |
| **Neutral**<br>Multiple uses. | 0 | 0 |
| **SOS or Win-Win**<br>Contracting out with rules. | ++ | ++ |

# Obtaining Private Land for Public Use:
# Compensation for Changing Land Use

The issue here is what compensation, if any, should a landowner receive as a result of a decrease in land value due to rezoning or land regulation. An example would be rezoning coastal land to prohibit new motels in order to provide for wetlands protection.

Conservatives want the landowner fully compensated for the loss in value even though landowners need not compensate the government when a rezoning goes in the opposite direction to increase land value.

Liberals want the landowner fully compensated for the market value of the property if the property is being taken for a public use. The market value can include reduced value due to rezoning or land regulation.

A compromise position might be for the government to pay 50 percent of the loss in value. This would provide more profit to landowners than 0 percent, but less than 100 percent. It would facilitate land use changes more than paying 100 percent, but less facilitating than only having to pay 0 percent on the loss.

**Table 6.7   Compensation for Land Use**

| | GOALS | |
| --- | --- | --- |
| **ALTERNATIVES** | **Conservative** <br> Protect the landowner. | **Liberal** <br> Facilitate land use for public interest. |
| **Conservative** <br> 100% pay for losses. | + | − |
| **Liberal** <br> 0% pay for losses. | − | + |
| **Neutral** <br> 50% pay for losses. | 0 | 0 |
| **SOS or Win-Win** <br> 0% pay for losses but only 50% of capital gains tax. | ++ | ++ |

A super-optimum solution might involve a statute that would provide for compensation at the market value (with 0 percent losses or gains due to rezoning) combined with a provision that requires paying only 50 percent of the capital gains tax. The landowner then makes a big profit after taxes, but the government that takes the land only has to pay its market value. It is easier for the federal government to forego some tax money than to have to make substantial extra payments. This could be combined with a revision of the capital gains tax to also provide for a tax reduction for productivity increases.

# Chapter 7

# Labor and Management

## The Minimum Wage Problem

### The Philippine Minimum Wage Problem

As of early 1991, management argued that the maximum it could afford was 90 pesos per day. Otherwise, workers would have to be laid off or not hired leading to a reduction in food, shelter, and clothing.

Labor argued that the minimum wage should be at least 100 pesos per day. Otherwise, workers would not be able to afford adequate food, shelter, and clothing.

**Table 7.1   The Philippine Minimum Wage Problem**

| | GOALS | |
|---|---|---|
| **ALTERNATIVES** | **Conservative** Overpayment. | **Liberal** Decent wages. |
| **Conservative** 90 per day. | + | − |
| **Liberal** 100 per day. | − | + |
| **Neutral** 95 per day. | 0 | 0 |
| **SOS or Win-Win** 101 to worker, 89 from employer, 12 wage supplement. | ++ | ++ |

The logical compromise would be somewhere between 90 and 100 pesos depending on the relative bargaining power of management and labor.

The SOS involves management paying 89 pesos, but the workers receiving 101 pesos. The government makes up the difference of 12 pesos per day in return for management and labor activities.

To receive the 12-peso subsidy, management must agree to hire only unemployed workers and provide them with on-the-job training to bring their skills up to the 101-peso level. The unemployed workers must accept the job and the OJT training, and perform both at a passing level.

## Using Minimum Wage Policy to Illustrate SOS Analysis

There are some relatively neutral goals that relate to saving taxes, employing the unemployed, providing on-the-job training, and providing positive adult role models. The main goals, however, are the conservative goal of avoiding overpayment of wages and the liberal goal of paying decent living wages.

## The Davis-Bacon Act

The Davis-Bacon Act provides that the prevailing union wage in a community must be paid to workers on federal projects. Conservatives would prefer to pay lower wages in order to promote higher profits. Liberals want to retain the Davis-Bacon system. A compromise would be to require at least 90 percent of the union wage or some percentage lower than 100 percent.

A SOS solution might be to retain the Davis-Bacon system, but provide federal subsidies to employers on such federal projects in order to upgrade the workers' skills or introduce new technologies. Doing so should increase worker productivity, and enable one worker to do the job of more than one worker. That has the effect of reducing the total wage bill per project and increasing profits without changing the Davis-Bacon Act. Job facilitators also need to be provided to displaced workers.

**Table 7.2   Davis-Bacon**

|  | GOALS | |
|---|---|---|
| **ALTERNATIVES** | **Conservative** High profits. | **Liberal** High wages. |
| **Conservative** Allow low wages on federal projects. | + | − |
| **Liberal** Require union wages on federal projects. | − | + |
| **Neutral** Require 90% of union wages. | 0 | 0 |
| **SOS or Win-Win** Increase productivity with federal aid. | ++ | ++ |

# Labor-Management Bargaining

## Resolving Litigation Disputes through Super-Optimum Solutions

If the defendant wins on trial, this benefits the defendant, but hurts the plaintiff. The defendant may also be hurt by the costs of the litigation.

If the plaintiff wins on trial, this benefits the plaintiff, but hurts the defendant. The plaintiff may also be hurt by the costs of the litigation.

If there is a monetary settlement, the defendant does not gain as much as in a defendant victory, and the plaintiff does not gain as much as in a plaintiff victory. Neither side, however, loses as much money as they would if the other side were to win.

**Table 7.3   Resolving Litigation**

|  | GOALS | |
| :--- | :--- | :--- |
| **ALTERNATIVES** | **Conservative**<br>Benefits to defendant. | **Liberal**<br>Benefits to plaintiff. |
| **Conservative**<br>Defendant wins on trials. | + | – |
| **Liberal**<br>Plaintiff wins on trials. | – | + |
| **Neutral**<br>Settle. | 0 | 0 |
| **SOS or Win-Win**<br>1. Insurance.<br>2. Products.<br>3. Credit unions. | ++ | ++ |

A SOS solution involves the defendant giving the plaintiff insurance, manufactured products, or other items that the defendant makes. Doing so may result in the plaintiff receiving things that are of more value to the plaintiff than the plaintiff's best expectations. Doing so may also result in the defendant giving things that are of less value to the defendant than the defendant's best expectations.

## Super-Optimizing Litigation Analysis
## (Using Ramirez v. Rousonelos as an Illustrative Example)

In Table 7.4 the plaintiff's wildest initial expectation is to be repaid approximately $1 million in wages. That is a wild expectation since the money was deducted for goods, services, and advances that had been provided to the workers by the grower, but not in accordance with the proper paperwork procedures.

The defendant's wildest initial expectation is to have to pay nothing. That is a wild expectation since the defendant admittedly failed to comply with the proper deduction procedures with no good defense other than that the money was owed. The defendant would thus be likely to lose on the issue of whether they complied with the proper procedures. A penalty is likely to be assessed to deter such improprieties on the part of the specific defendant and other potential defendants. The penalty is likely to be substantial in order to have deterrent value. There is also likely to be compensation to the named defendants for their efforts plus considerable litigation costs if the case goes to trial.

The object is thus to arrive at a super-optimum solution whereby the workers in a sense receive more than $1 million and the defendant pays nothing.

The key element in the super-optimum solution is the establishment of a credit union mainly consisting of $100,000 from the defendant to be deposited with interest for five years.

That $100,000 can quickly generate $7 million worth of housing by serving as a 10 percent down payment on a mortgage for existing or new housing units for the workers. The housing might be used as collateral for additional capital. It is also possible that a federal or

**Table 7.4    Ramirez**

|  | GOALS | |
|---|---|---|
| | **Conservative** | **Liberal** |
| | Little money to | Big money to |
| **ALTERNATIVES** | plaintiff. | plaintiff. |
| **Conservative** <br> Defendant's best expectation = $0. | + | − |
| **Liberal** <br> Plaintiff's best expectation = $1,000. | − | + |
| **Neutral** <br> Likely compromise settlement = $500. | 0 | 0 |
| **SOS or Win-Win** <br> 1. Credit union, housing, and business opportunities. <br> 2. Grievance procedures. <br> 3. Payment to named plaintiff. <br> 4. Compliance information. <br> 5. Thus, big benefits for plaintiff and low cost to defendant. | ++ | ++ |

*Note: Ramirez v. Rousonelos* was a 1980 case involving a leading grower in Peoria, Illinois, who was sued by the Migrant Legal Counsel.

state government agency will match the $100,000 as part of an economic development plan, thereby further increasing the lending opportunities.

The workers thereby obtain multiple family housing and a lending source for business opportunities that may be worth at least $2 million plus the benefits of an improved grievance procedures, payment to named plaintiffs, and compliance information. The total value is worth more than their wildest best expectation.

The growers thereby obtain the benefits of not having to provide housing for the workers. They also get interest on their savings and a subsequent return of the principal if requested. The grievance procedure can decrease friction. The compliance information can increase credibility. Payment to the named plaintiffs is a cost rather than a benefit, but it is more than offset by the benefits from the other relevant items of value. Therefore the growers are making a net gain as a result of this SOS settlement which is the same as paying nothing.

# Overseas Labor Problems

### The Asian Labor Shortage

Business conservatives welcome cheap labor to decrease their expenses and increase their profits. Cultural conservatives resist easy immigration as being disruptive to national purity.

Union liberals resist immigration as being disruptive to union wages. Intellectual liberals like to provide ambitious immigrants with opportunities to succeed.

By relieving the labor shortage, immigration increases the gross national product. There is, however, some disruption in absorbing the new immigrants.

The SOS alternative involves increasing the labor force by upgrading the skills of the elderly, the disabled, and mothers of preschool children. It also makes better use of people who work part-time or seasonally, or who could use a second or better job and increases the productivity of present workers through new technologies and training.

**Table 7.5   Asian Labor Shortage**

| ALTERNATIVES | GOALS | |
| --- | --- | --- |
| | Conservative<br>Increase GNP. | Liberal<br>Decrease disruption<br>to society. |
| **Conservative**<br>1. Import cheap labor.<br>2. Preserve national purity. | + | − |
| **Liberal**<br>1. Preserve union wages.<br>2. Provide immigrant opportunities. | − | + |
| **Neutral**<br>Settle. | 0 | 0 |
| **SOS or Win-Win**<br>1. Increase labor force.<br>2. Increase productivity. | ++ | ++ |

## Handwork versus Assembly Lines in India Clothmaking

The conservative Gandhi position is to emphasize handcrafted work. Doing so may not be high in productivity, but it provides quality workplaces in terms of safety, dignity, and being free of pollution.

The liberalized position is to emphasize assembly-line work associated with industrialized societies. Doing so may be high in productivity, but often lacks safety, dignity, and cleanliness.

The compromise is working at home but with machines that work off electric outlets. Such machines are more productive than handlooms while at the same time not so unsafe, undignified, or unclean as factories.

The SOS alternative might be to have highly automated assembly plants like Japan. Such plants do even better on productivity than traditional assembly lines, and generally better on safety, dignity, and cleanliness than electric machines.

**Table 7.6   Indian Clothmaking (Handwork versus Assembly Lines)**

| ALTERNATIVES | GOALS | |
| --- | --- | --- |
| | **Conservative**<br>Productivity. | **Liberal**<br>Quality workplace. |
| **Conservative**<br>Hand-crafted work. | + | – |
| **Liberal**<br>Assembly line work. | – | + |
| **Neutral**<br>Cottage industries with<br>small machines. | 0 | 0 |
| **SOS or Win-Win**<br>Highly automated assem-<br>bly plant. | ++ | ++ |

# Labor Standards and Unions

### Evaluating Labor-Management Policies

Workplace in this context refers to safety, minimum wages, maximum hours, child labor, environmental protection, and non-discrimination.

Union in this context refers to the right to join a union without being fired, the right to collectively bargain, the right to strike, and other rules that increase the ability of unions to more effectively represent workers.

Working together refers to labor and management seeking to increase productivity through new technologies, on-the-job training, and incentives that are mutually arrived at.

### Relating Labor Policies to Societal Goals

Reduced profits is a short-run effect of policies to reduce abuse of workers. Increased profits is a long-run effect since such policies stimulate the adoption of labor-saving equipment which tends to

**Table 7.7 Labor Management**

| | GOALS | |
| | Conservative<br>Stimulate business. | Liberal<br>1. Protect workers.<br>2. Equity. |
| **ALTERNATIVES** | | |
| --- | --- | --- |
| **Conservative**<br>1. Decrease workplace.<br>2. Decrease union. | + | – |
| **Liberal**<br>1. Increase workplace.<br>2. Increase union. | – | + |
| **Neutral**<br>1. Some union<br>    restrictions.<br>2. Some management<br>    restrictions. | **0** | **0** |
| **SOS or Win-Win**<br>1. Working together.<br>2. On-the-job training. | ++ | ++ |

increase productivity and profitability.

Increased taxes is frequently a short-run effect of new government policies, but not as much policies that regulate, as contrasted to those that subsidize. Decreased taxes may be the indirect or long-run effect if the regulation results in enabling workers to be healthier and more productive and less likely to become welfare dependents, especially due to premature aging or disability.

All of the goals are stated in a positive way so that a plus on the taxpayer's goal means a favorable effect from the taxpayer's perspective, rather than an increase in the taxpayer's burden.

All the policies in the above table seem to cross a minimum threshold of desirability. By that we mean that the conservative policies toward labor that are listed here are mainstream policies rather than extremist policies. We do not include extreme reactionary policies like slavery, serfdom, peonage, or prohibiting the existence of unions. Likewise, on the liberal side, we do not include extreme radical policies like exterminating employers or running all businesses as employee cooperatives.

## Table 7.8 Labor Policies

| | GOALS | |
| --- | --- | --- |
| **ALTERNATIVES** | **Conservative**<br>1. Stimulate business.<br>2. Reduce burden on taxpayers. | **Liberal**<br>1. Reduce abuse of workers.<br>2. Consumers on price and quality. |
| **Conservative**<br>1. No union abuses in management.<br>2. No union abuses in members.<br>3. Delayed emergency strikes. | + | − |
| **Liberal**<br>1. Maximum hours.<br>2. Maximum wages, including supplements.<br>3. No child labor.<br>4. No discrimination.<br>5. No safety abuses.<br>6. No management abuse of unions. | − | + |
| **Neutral**<br>In between or some of both. | 0 | 0 |
| **SOS or Win-Win**<br>See text. | ++ | ++ |

# Striker Replacement

## Permanent Striker Replacements

The National Labor Relations Act of 1993 allows employers to permanently replace strikers. The Clinton administration has proposed to amend the act to ban such permanent replacements, although still allowing temporary replacements.

The neutral or compromise position is to encourage mediation to prevent or resolve strikes. It may also allow for permanent replace-

**Table 7.9 Striker Replacement**

| | GOALS | |
|---|---|---|
| **ALTERNATIVES** | **Conservative**<br>Increase profits. | **Liberal**<br>Increase wages. |
| **Conservative**<br>Allow replacements. | + | − |
| **Liberal**<br>Ban replacements. | − | + |
| **Neutral**<br>Mediation. | 0 | 0 |
| **SOS or Win-Win**<br>Increase productivity. | ++ | ++ |

ment after a long time period, but that could cause management to stall until the time period passes while still giving the appearance of bargaining.

Mediation can include the calling of an election whereby the workers can choose: (1) to accept management's last offer, (2) reject the offer and continue negotiating, but return to work, or (3) reject the offer, not return to work, and take a chance that permanent replacements will be found. In the absence of such an election, management may exaggerate the support it has among workers, and the union leaders may exaggerate the militancy of the workers.

The SOS solution might be to increase worker productivity through new technologies and the upgrading of skills. Doing so can both increase profits more than allowing replacements, and can increase wages more than banning replacements. An increase in productivity can also increase sales by allowing for price reductions due to lower labor expense and improved product quality due to better manufacturing processes and more skilled workers.

## A SOS Analysis of Some Aspects of
## Federal Aviation Administration Policy

Table 7.10 represents a SOS analysis of the labor-management dispute between the Federal Aviation Administration and the Flight Controllers Union during the first term of the Reagan administration.

The conservative alternative was mainly to reduce the wage demands of the flight controllers by locking them out or replacing them if necessary. The liberal alternative was to consider the wage demands of the flight controllers to be reasonable and to therefore pay them. The neutral position was somewhere between what the agency was offering and what the union was demanding.

A key conservative goal was to keep down the costs to the airlines who would have to pay for some of the wage increases by way of increased airport fees. Conservatives were also concerned with keeping down the costs to the taxpayers. Liberals argued in favor of higher wages in order to compensate the workers for the stressful nature of the work. Liberals also advocated the buying of expensive equipment that would enable the workers to do their jobs with less stress and more safety.

A SOS alternative might have various components. One might be to provide the workers with more benefits that do not involve increased wages such as shorter hours and more days off to relieve some of the stress of the work. A second component would be to

**Table 7.10      Federal Aviation Administration**

|  | GOALS | |
| --- | --- | --- |
| **ALTERNATIVES** | **Conservative**<br>Decrease airline $. | **Liberal**<br>Safety. |
| **Conservative**<br>Reduce labor and equipment<br>cost. | + | – |
| **Liberal**<br>Pay high labor and equipment<br>cost. | – | + |
| **Neutral**<br>In between. | 0 | 0 |
| **SOS or Win-Win**<br>1. Non-wage benefits.<br>2. Subsidy for high safety and<br>   low cost systems. | ++ | ++ |

subsidize new traffic control systems that would be safer and less stressful, but also less labor intensive thereby resulting in some layoffs. A third component might be a program to develop new skills for those flight controllers who might be laid off so they could obtain reasonably good jobs elsewhere.

The idea of new technologies that can increase benefits and reduce costs is an important type of SOS solution. Adopting it may, however, require special retraining for workers who are displaced by such new technologies. They are like workers displaced as a result of lowering of tariffs or facilitating new entries into the labor force.

## Upgrading Labor Skills

The Clinton administration is proposing a retraining program for American workers. It involves the same kind of issues of universal coverage, alternative delivery systems, and payment options that the health plan also involves.

Conservatives emphasize leaving training to individual workers and firms rather than having the government adopt large-scale training programs. Their key goal seems to be to save tax money.

Liberals advocate special government training programs for the unemployed, including the elderly, the disabled, mothers of preschool children, and the people in the labor force who are unable to find jobs–such as workers who are displaced by new technologies, lowering tariffs, immigration, and conversion to peacetime production.

The neutral position would involve an appropriation that is somewhere between very little (as advocated by conservatives) and very much (as advocated by liberals).

A SOS alternative might include everyone in the labor force in order to increase total productivity, the GNP, national spending, and new jobs which come from new spending. The idea is that unemployed workers will benefit more from an increase in jobs in the economy for which they can apply or be trained, than they will from receiving training for jobs that are not so available.

A SOS alternative would emphasize on-the-job training and

**Table 7.11    Upgrading Labor**

| | GOALS | |
|---|---|---|
| **ALTERNATIVES** | **Conservative**<br>Save tax money. | **Liberal**<br>Upgrade skills. |
| **Conservative**<br>Leave to individual worker<br>and firms. | + | – |
| **Liberal**<br>Special government training<br>for unemployed. | – | + |
| **Neutral**<br>In-between appropriation. | **0** | **0** |
| **SOS or Win-Win**<br>1. Everyone in labor force.<br>2. On-the-job training for job-<br>    based training.<br>3. Refundable 1% payroll tax. | ++ | ++ |

training toward specific available jobs. The delivery system would thus be the businesses that are doing the hiring, rather than training by government agencies or by schools separate from the businesses which provide jobs.

The financing might come from a 1 percent payroll tax that is refundable if the businesses use the money for upgrading skills of present or incoming workers.

# Chapter 8

# Capital, Business, and Consumers

## Business-Consumer Relations

### Evaluating Policies for Business-Consumer Relations

Having an unregulated marketplace may stimulate business, but it does not do so well on protecting the consumer, especially if the marketplace results in a few non-competing firms.

**Table 8.1 (New) Business-Consumer**

| | GOALS | |
|---|---|---|
| **ALTERNATIVES** | **Conservative**<br>1. Stimulate business.<br>2. Decrease tax burden short term. | **Liberal**<br>1. Protect consumer.<br>2. Equity. |
| **Conservative**<br>Do nothing. | + | − |
| **Liberal**<br>Government ownership. | − | + |
| **Neutral**<br>1. Regulated economy.<br>2. Mixed economy. | 0 | 0 |
| **SOS or Win-Win**<br>1. Marketplace with subsidies.<br>2. Tax breaks.<br>3. Contracting out. | ++ | ++ |

Government ownership may be more sensitive to consumers as voters, but government ownership tends to mean monopolies that lack efficiency.

A regulated mixed economy scores between the conservative and liberal alternatives on stimulating business and protecting consumers from products that may be unsafe, untruthfully advertised, or overpriced.

Business can be stimulated even more through well-placed subsidies and tax breaks–especially seed money to encourage new competing businesses–and contracting out to competing businesses what might otherwise be government activities.

## Alternative Public Policies for Business-Consumer Relations

The overall conclusion to be drawn from Table 8.2 is that each policy has its place:

1. Doing nothing works best where marketplace competition provides consumer benefits and productivity incentives, as with airline deregulation.
2. Government aid works best where private enterprise cannot raise enough large long-term capital to take advantage of the potential of technological innovation
3. Litigation works best to provide injured individuals with compensation, but is generally not as good a preventive approach as regulation is.
4. Regulation works best where the marketplace cannot adequately protect the consumer, as with products that do not have brand names but could be unsafe.
5. Government ownership works best for essential industries where the public demands equity but private enterprise cannot profitably provide the service under an equitable arrangement.

**Table 8.2   (Old) Business-Consumer**

| ALTERNATIVES | GOALS | |
|---|---|---|
| | **Conservative**<br>1. Stimulate business to greater productivity.<br>2. Taxpayer expense. | **Liberal**<br>1. Protect consumer.<br>2. Equity. |
| **Conservative**<br>1. Do nothing.<br>2. Government aid and sub-<br>   sidies. | + | − |
| **Liberal**<br>1. Government ownership.<br>2. Regulation. | − | + |
| **Neutral**<br>Litigation. | 0 | 0 |
| **SOS or Win-Win**<br>1. Government aid.<br>2. Subsidies. | ++ | ++ |

The score of a policy on a goal may depend on greater details than are provided on the table. For example, the extent to which government ownership is protective of consumers depends on whether the government base is democratic or dictatorial.

# Business in Developing Nations

## Selling Polish Corporate Stock to Foreigners

Table 8.3 was developed along with some Polish economists at a United Nations conference in Geneva in 1988 dealing with training people for new economic relations.

The hardline conservatives wanted stock to only be sold to Polish citizens. The more liberal types wanted stock to be sold to anyone. The compromise position was allow stock in Polish corporations to be sold to outsiders up to about 50 percent of the stock in a corporation. That would obtain some outside capital without having full outside control.

**Table 8.3    Polish Corporate Stock**

|  | GOALS | |
| --- | --- | --- |
| **ALTERNATIVES** | **Conservative** Avoid foreign exploitation. | **Liberal** Get capital for development. |
| **Conservative** Retain stock in Poland. | + | − |
| **Liberal** Let all buy. | − | + |
| **Neutral** Up to 49%. | 0 | 0 |
| **SOS or Win-Win** 1. Poland retains little. 2. Leases to corporate entrepreneurs. | ++ | ++ |

The SOS alternative is to retain ownership by the Polish govern-ment but lease the operation of all corporations to the highest-bidding entrepreneurs within Poland or elsewhere. Doing so is a form of contracting out that can result in much foreign input while at the same time retaining Polish control.

**Business Development and Africa**

Liberals tend to like small, family businesses. Conservatives tend to like larger, less personal businesses.

It is possible to emphasize small businesses at first since they are more feasible, but to emphasize those more likely to lead to larger businesses that will employ more people. Such businesses may emphasize manufacturing products, rather than retailing food or clothing. This SOS is an example of sequential compatibility.

**Table 8.4    Business Development and Africa**

| ALTERNATIVES | GOALS | |
| --- | --- | --- |
| | **Conservative**<br>Easy feasibility. | **Liberal**<br>Value to economy. |
| **Conservative**<br>Large business. | + | – |
| **Liberal**<br>Small business | – | + |
| **Neutral**<br>Medium business. | 0 | 0 |
| **SOS or Win-Win**<br>Small to large (especially<br>manufacturing). | ++ | ++ |

## Blacks versus Browns in Africa Retailing

Table 8.5 refers to Africanization in East Africa including Nairobi, Kenya. The pro-business alternative is to not interfere with the fact that the businesses were dominated by people from India and Pakistan as of the 1960s.

The liberal alternative may go so far as to require ownership to be in the hands of black Africans, rather than brown Asians.

The neutral alternative might be to help blacks acquire businesses by lending them money, but not go so far as to require black ownership.

The conservative alternative may be good for black consumers if the brown business people can operate more efficiently. The liberal alternative may be good for would-be black business people.

The reality is that untrained blacks lacking an entrepreneurial tradition tend to stay in business for a relatively short time. Thus the Nairobi shopping area went from brown to black between 1960 and 1970, but then it went back to brown between 1970 and 1980.

The SOS alternative might involve upgrading the skills of those who aspire to operate businesses so they can have better ability to persevere and to provide better service to the black consumers.

**Table 8.5    Blacks versus Browns in Africa**

| ALTERNATIVES | GOALS | |
| --- | --- | --- |
| | **Conservative** Upgrade black consumers. | **Liberal** Upgrade black business people. |
| **Conservative** Browns dominate. | + | − |
| **Liberal** Blacks dominate. | − | + |
| **Neutral** Help blacks. | 0 | 0 |
| **SOS or Win-Win** Upgrade skills. | ++ | ++ |

# Specific Types of Business

## Cable TV

The conservative alternative on the economics of cable TV is to have no price regulation, but instead leave it up to the marketplace. Conservatives may, however, be divided as to whether they endorse anti-trust activities to promote competition among cable TV companies. The liberal alternative tends to emphasize price regulation, especially where the pricing might otherwise be monopolistic. The neutral position is somewhere between the high prices of an unregulated monopolistic market and the low prices that would be imposed by liberal legislation.

The main conservative goal is to allow businesses to profit on the theory that the profit motive leads to better products, although that may assume a competitive marketplace. The main liberal goal is quality service at low prices to consumers. In this context, there is no issue as to whether cable TV should be regulated regarding its contents. Only the economic aspects are being considered here.

**Table 8.6   Cable TV**

| | GOALS | |
| | Conservative | Liberal |
| ALTERNATIVES | Profit to business. | Service to customers. |
| --- | --- | --- |
| **Conservative**<br>No regulation. | + | − |
| **Liberal**<br>Regulation. | − | + |
| **Neutral**<br>Some regulation. | 0 | 0 |
| **SOS or Win-Win**<br>Contract out to 2 or more<br>(with open use clause). | ++ | ++ |

A super-optimum solution might provide even more profit to business than the unregulated monopolistic firm and better service to consumers than regulation can provide. This can be brought about through contracting out by the city government where the cable TV is located.

The contracting out would be to two or more firms with a requirement that they rent their cable lines to each other at a reasonable profit. If one firm was previously generating 100 units of profit and now two firms are generating 120 units of profit, then total profit has increased even though each firm may be making less profit than the one previously monopolistic firm.

The contracting out should improve service to consumers by virtue of the competition among the cable TV firms to obtain one of the government contracts. There would also be competition among the two or more winning firms since they would each be partly competing in the same market. Potential customers would be aware of the rates and services of each firm.

## Commissions, Salaries, and Consumer Protection

Table 8.7 was suggested by news reports that the Prudential

brokerage firm had swindled its customers out of billions of dollars by lying to them regarding stocks that Prudential was selling. The Security and Exchange Commission negotiated a settlement to compensate customers who had suffered losses. ("U.S. Judge Approves a Prudential Settlement" in *New York Times*, 18 November 1995, p. 36.)

The argument was that paying brokers a percentage of the fees they collect causes them to encourage people to engage in transactions contrary to their best interests, but which will generate commissions. This is almost like the old justice-of-the-peace system where judges were paid a percentage of the fines they levied or damages they awarded.

The commission system does not promote sales. It can be contrasted with a salary system which provides less of an incentive, although salaries include differential starting salaries and raises to reward future or past sales. The salary system is less likely to result in consumer abuse. There is some consumer concern, even under the commission system in order to get repeat customers.

A SOS system that promotes sales and protects customers might be a combination of salary and profit shares, as is done in HMOs and law partnerships. The profit shares can be allocated by considering reasonably clear criteria that relate one's contributions to the medical clinic or law firm.

**Table 8.7   Commissions and Salaries**

|  | GOALS | |
| --- | --- | --- |
| **ALTERNATIVES** | **Conservative**<br>Promote sales. | **Liberal**<br>Consumer protection. |
| **Conservative**<br>Commission. | + | − |
| **Liberal**<br>Salary. | − | + |
| **Neutral**<br>Both. | 0 | 0 |
| **SOS or Win-Win**<br>Salary and profit sharing. | ++ | ++ |

There is a question as to how the combination of salary and profit shares can be encouraged by public policy. There are laws that relate to minimum wages and non-discrimination in wages, but not requirements that relate to commissions versus salaries. Perhaps the best public policy is to encourage competition in order to get the businesses to adopt internal rules that are good for both sales and consumer protection. The suggestion has been made of allowing banks to sell stocks and bonds as good competition for stock brokerage firms in order to change their heavy emphasis on commissions.

# PART THREE

# TECHNOLOGY POLICY

# Section A

# Improving Urban and Regional Planning

# Chapter 9

# Environmental Protection

## Incentives for Reducing Pollution

### Alternative Ways of Dealing with the Problem of Pollution

At first glance, the analysis in Table 9.1 appears to lead to a three-way tie. However, at second glance, the analysis indicates that relying on the marketplace doe not satisfy a minimum level of pollution-reduction because neither private firms nor municipalities have an incentive to reduce pollution since doing so will mean an increase in expenses with no increase in income. The analysis also indicates that relying on pollution taxes (that are proportionate to the amount of pollution generated) does not satisfy a minimum level of political feasibility, because pollution taxes generate too much opposition

**Table 9.1    (Old) Pollution**

|  | GOALS | |
| --- | --- | --- |
| **ALTERNATIVES** | **Conservative** Political feasibility. | **Liberal** Pollution reduction. |
| **Conservative** Marketplace. | + | − |
| **Liberal** Regulation. | − | + |
| **Neutral** | 0 | 0 |
| **SOS or Win-Win** Pollution taxes. | ++ | ++ |

from private firms and municipalities. This leads to the conclusion that regulation is the best alternative for dealing with pollution, including a system of permits, inspection, and prosecution for violating the permits granted.

This analysis is an example of minimum constraints on the goals, as contrasted to minimum constraints on the alternatives.

One might also note that in this substantive context, the bottom line as to who wins is insensitive to the weights of the goals or the measurement categories, since only one alternative meets the minimum constraints. For example, suppose pollution reduction is scored 2, 4, and 5 on marketplace, regulation, and pollution taxes. Suppose further that political feasibility is scored 4, 4, and 3. One would still arrive at the same conclusion that regulation is the best alternative if one requires better than a 2 on pollution reduction and better than a 3 on political feasibility.

The political feasibility scores shown in the above table are as of about 1970 when water and air pollution legislation was first being proposed at the federal level. As of 1987, the political feasibility of going to a total marketplace solution should be substantially lower since it would mean repealing existing federal regulation. As of 1987, pollution taxes are even more politically unfeasible as a result of observing how they have been defeated at the federal, state, and local levels.

There are many more alternatives for dealing with the problem of pollution than just the marketplace, regulation, and pollution taxes. See the more detailed Table 9.2 entitled "(Old) Incentives for Reducing Pollution" which contains nineteen alternatives that lend themselves to various combinations including the alternative of selling and buying marketable pollution rights which in effect combines policies of relying on the marketplace, regulation, and pollution taxes.

## Comparing Alternative Incentives for Reducing Pollution

Subsidies to provide rewards or reduce costs can be effective, but they are expensive. These are subsidies mainly to businesses to encourage the adoption of devices to reduce the impact of pollution. More effective subsidies go to research entities to develop new methods for reducing the occurrence of pollution while keeping manufacturing costs down.

Reward subsidies cover more than just costs, whereas cost subsidies only cover all or part of the costs.

**Table 9.2    (Old) Incentives for Reducing Pollution**

| | GOALS | |
| --- | --- | --- |
| | **Conservative**<br>1. Cost to general public.<br>2. Predictability and due process. | **Liberal**<br>1. Effectiveness in reducing pollution.<br>2. Clean up funds.<br>3. Cost to consumers or workers.<br>4. Public participation. |
| **ALTERNATIVES** | | |
| **Conservative**<br>1. Increase benefits or right doing.<br>2. Reward subsidies to cities.<br>3. Reward subsidies to business.<br>4. Pollution tax reduction.<br>5. New government contracts.<br>6. Selling marketable pollution rights. | + | − |
| **Liberal**<br>1. Increase cost of wrongdoing.<br>2. Damage suits.<br>3. Pollution tax.<br>4. Fines.<br>5. Jail.<br>6. Loss of government contracts.<br>7. Buying marketable pollution rights.<br>8. Padlock injunction.<br>9. Reduce benefits of wrongdoing.<br>10. Confiscate profits. | − | + |
| **Neutral**<br>1. Increase probability of benefits and costs.<br>2. Improve monitoring.<br>3. Bounties for reporting. | 0 | 0 |
| **SOS or Win-Win**<br>Do all. | ++ | ++ |

Damage suits are difficult to win. Fines and jail sentences are difficult to impose. Pollution taxes are quite difficult to get adopted. Padlock injunctions may cause undesirable unemployment. Loss of government contracts is not much of a threat if one does not already have government contracts. Publicizing wrongdoers does not help when they do not sell to ultimate consumers, and even the consumers are more influenced by other considerations.

The government can issue marketable pollution rights. Firms that pollute relatively little will then have an excess of rights to sell to firms that produce relatively a lot. The high prices they charge provide an incentive to reduce pollution.

Any item that is negative on political feasibility is probably not worth emphasizing. The alternatives that are politically feasible do seem worth adopting along with subsidies to develop less expensive and cleaner manufacturing processes.

## Evaluating Incentives for Reducing Pollution

The alternatives that score relatively high include:

1. Giving government contracts to business firms that satisfy or excel on meeting pollution requirements.
2. The pollution tax system although it may not be able to meet a minimum political feasibility level.
3. The buying and selling of marketable pollution rights as a cost to polluters and an income reward for non-polluters.
4. Bounties for reporting wrongdoing whereby the general public shares in fines that are levied.

The alternatives that score relative low include:

1. Reward subsidies to business are opposed as being too expensive to the taxpayer.
2. Fines tend to be treated as a petty business expenses that are passed on to taxpayers.

## Table 9.3 (New) Incentives for Reducing Pollution

| | GOALS | |
|---|---|---|
| **ALTERNATIVES** | **Conservative**<br>Stimulate business. | **Liberal**<br>1. Effectiveness in decreasing pollution.<br>2. Clean up funds.<br>3. Cost to consumers or workers. |
| **Conservative**<br>1. Increase benefits of right doing.<br>2. Reward subsidies to cities.<br>3. Reward subsidies to business.<br>4. Pollution tax reduction.<br>5. New government contracts.<br>6. Selling marketable pollution rights.<br>7. Reducing costs of right doing: tax deductions.<br>8. Cost subsidies to cities.<br>9. Cost subsidies to business. | + | – |
| **Liberal**<br>1. Increase cost of wrongdoing.<br>2. Damage suits.<br>3. Publicize wrongdoers.<br>4. Fines.<br>5. Jail.<br>6. Loss of government contracts.<br>7. Buying marketable pollution rights.<br>8. Padlock injunction.<br>9. Reduce benefits of wrongdoing.<br>10. Confiscate profits. | – | + |
| **Neutral**<br>1. Increase probability of benefits and costs.<br>2. Improve monitoring.<br>3. Bounties for reporting. | 0 | 0 |
| **SOS or Win-Win**<br>Combine all. | ++ | ++ |

3. Jail sentences are unlikely to be imposed and thus relatively ineffective.
4. Padlock injunctions that are opposed because they result in loss of employment and production.

If the criteria are going to be weighted differently, political feasibility can be considered a constraint such that any alternative with a double-minus is considered unfeasible. Of the other criteria, effectiveness in reducing pollution is probably the most important, followed by cost to the general taxpayers.

The alternatives relate to incentives for reducing pollution. One could do a similar analysis concerning government structures for reducing pollution. The structural alternatives might be divided into those that relate to federalism, separation of powers, and relations between government and people.

Predictability and due process are neutral goals in the sense that they are about equally supported by conservatives and liberals. Predictability in this context tends to refer to the extent to which formulas are followed for determining who gets benefits or costs. Due process refers to the extent to which the alternatives allow for those who are denied benefits or made to bear costs to receive a formal hearing to show they are being wrongly treated.

## Evaluating Policies for Dealing with Pollution

Conservatives prefer state regulation, rather than federal regulation because the states are more oriented toward promoting local business interests.

Conservatives prefer the courts over administrative agencies for regulation purposes since the legal rules and the generalist nature of the courts make them less effective than specialized more flexible administrative agencies.

Marketable pollution rights allow polluting businesses to buy pollution rights from other businesses in order to satisfy federal requirements. The high prices charged served as an incentive to reduce some pollution.

**Table 9.4　Evaluating Policies for Dealing with Pollution**

| ALTERNATIVES | GOALS | |
|---|---|---|
| | **Conservative**<br>Stimulate business. | **Liberal**<br>1. Reduce pollution.<br>2. Equity. |
| **Conservative**<br>1. Marketplace.<br>2. States.<br>3. Courts. | + | − |
| **Liberal**<br>1. Regulation, federal<br>　government.<br>2. Administrative<br>　agencies. | − | + |
| **Neutral**<br>Regulate toxic wastes. | 0 | 0 |
| **SOS or Win-Win**<br>1. Marketable pollution<br>　rights.<br>2. Subsidies. | ++ | ++ |

Subsidies in this context tend to refer to subsidizing a business firm or a municipality to buy devices that reduce pollution such as chimney or spigot filters. The subsidies may also be given to the filter manufacturers. These are different subsidies than those designed to develop manufacturing processes that are both less expensive and cleaner.

## A SOS Analysis of Economic Development versus a Clean Environment in Developing Nations

Improved processes refer to those that cost less and thereby facilitate greater profits, while at the same time being cleaner for environmental protection.

That may require a well-placed government subsidy to university engineering departments or other research institutes to develop such processes.

## Table 9.5  Development versus a Clean Environment

| | GOALS | |
| :--- | :--- | :--- |
| **ALTERNATIVES** | **Conservative**<br>Rapid economic<br>development. | **Liberal**<br>Clean environment. |
| **Conservative**<br>Unregulated economic<br>development. | + | − |
| **Liberal**<br>Anti-pollution<br>regulations. | − | + |
| **Neutral**<br>Compromise regulations. | 0 | 0 |
| **SOS or Win-Win**<br>1. Improved<br>   manufacturing.<br>2. Agricultural processes. | ++ | ++ |


## Table 9.6  Archer Daniels Midland

| | GOALS | |
| :--- | :--- | :--- |
| **ALTERNATIVES** | **Conservative**<br>1. Preserve employment.<br>2. Tax base. | **Liberal**<br>Reduce pollution. |
| **Conservative**<br>Marketplace. | + | − |
| **Liberal**<br>Punish business<br>wrongdoing. | − | + |
| **Neutral**<br>Exceptions. | 0 | 0 |
| **SOS or Win-Win**<br>Develop new technologies<br>that are both more profitable<br>and cleaner. | ++ | ++ |

**Dealing with the Pollution of Archer Daniels Midland**

The components of the SOS package might include:

1. Improve the manufacturing process to reduce pollution and simultaneously reduce expenses that makes
   the business more profitable.
2. Find commercial by-products for the undesirable
   waste.
3. Better communicate the non-toxic nature of the pollution, but still reduce or eliminate their smell.

# Levels and Branches of Government in Pollution Policy

### Evaluating Levels of Government for Dealing with Pollution

The conservative alternative emphasizes state-level control,
whereas the liberal alternative emphasizes national-level control. The
state level is more sensitive to business profits, but the national level
is more sensitive to a clean environment. The SOS alternative is to
subsidize new technologies that will provide both a cleaner
environment and greater business profits simultaneously.

The winning liberal alternative is control by the national
government since it is less subject to influence by businesses or
municipal governments. The winning conservative alternative is
control by decentralized field offices and interstate compacts. State
agencies would do better on the conservative totals if business profits
were the main conservative goal.

Conservatives tend to endorse state rather than national environmental policy, because the states are more sensitive to local business
concerns. Liberals tend to endorse national policy, because the federal
government is less sensitive to local business concerns.

Neutral positions include: (1) decentralized federal field offices,
(2) interstate compacts and commissions, (3) rule-making at the
federal level but enforcement at the state level, (4) federal regulation

of new facilities but state regulation for old facilities, and (5) federal policy for air pollution, but state policy for water pollution.

Some conservatives might prefer no regulation at all rather than state regulation, but no regulation is not politically feasible. Liberals might prefer equally strong regulation at both the national and state levels, but that is probably not politically feasible for most states.

The SOS position is to subsidize new technologies that are both cleaner and more profitable. In the meantime, various incentive systems can be adopted to reward businesses for decreasing pollution and penalize them for not doing so. An example would be giving marketable pollution rights to low-polluting businesses, which have to be bought expensively by firms that do not reduce their pollution.

**Table 9.7   Levels of Government and Pollution**

| ALTERNATIVES | GOALS | |
|---|---|---|
| | **Conservative** Sensitivity to local factors. | **Liberal** Less business influence. |
| **Conservative** All state and local government. | + | − |
| **Liberal** All national government. | − | + |
| **Neutral** 1. Decentralized field offices. 2. Interstate compacts and commissions. 3. Rules for federal enforcement for states. 4. Federal new facilities. 5. State for old facilities. 6. Federal for air pollution. 7. State for water pollution. | 0 | 0 |
| **SOS or Win-Win** See text. | ++ | ++ |

**Evaluating Branches of Government for Dealing with Pollution**

Judicial emphasis does especially well on adjudicative due process and independence of political pressure. Legislative emphasis does especially well on legislative due process and responsiveness to public opinion. Administrative emphasis does especially well on specialized expertise, full-time concern, taking initiative, and acting flexibly.

Administrative emphasis does well on all three totals because it does well on so many of the individual criteria shown. If we were to add a criterion of minimizing the effective pressure on businesses, then the administrative emphasis would not do so well.

If one starts with the assumption of wanting to reduce pollution and of having to choose among judicial, legislative, and administrative emphasis, then combining all three approaches would be the most effective since they are not mutually exclusive. That means obtaining favorable anti-pollution decisions from courts, legislatures, and administrative agencies.

**Table 9.8    Branches of Government**

|  | GOALS | |
| --- | --- | --- |
|  | **Conservative**<br>1. Adjudicative due process.<br>2. Legislative due process. | **Liberal**<br>1. Specialized expertise.<br>2. Full time concern.<br>3. Take initiative, act flexibly. |
| **ALTERNATIVES** | | |
| **Conservative**<br>Judicial emphasis. | + | – |
| **Liberal**<br>Administrative emphasis. | – | + |
| **Neutral**<br>Legislative emphasis. | 0 | 0 |
| **SOS or Win-Win**<br>See text. | ++ | ++ |

Conservatives tend to endorse the courts and legislatures as sources of environmental policy and enforcement because they tend to be more subject to delay and manipulation by business interests.

Liberals tend to endorse administrative agencies as sources of environmental policy and enforcement because they do well on specialized expertise, full-time concern, taking the initiative, and acting flexibly.

Neutral positions allow for relevant administrative agencies, but subject to overruling by legislatures on their quasi-legislative activities, and overruling by the courts on their quasi-judicial activities.

Some conservatives might prefer no regulation at all or a substantial reduction, regardless of which branch of government is involved, but that may not be politically feasible. Liberals might prefer equally strong regulation from all three branches of government, but the severity of the regulation is limited by due process requirements and the influence of strong interest groups.

The SOS position is to subsidize new technologies that are both cleaner and more profitable. In the meantime, various incentive systems can be adopted to reward businesses for decreasing pollution and penalize them for not doing so. An example would be giving marketable pollution rights to low-polluting businesses, which have to be bought expensively by firms that do not reduce their pollution.

## International Environmental Protection

### Global Pollution and Super-Optimum Solutions

Global pollution mainly includes global warming and the lessening of the ozone layer. Global warming is largely attributed to the burning of fossil fuels like oil and coal, rather than cleaner fuels. The consequence might be to melt some of the arctic icecap and thereby cause a raising of the ocean level. Another consequence might be increasing the average temperatures in areas with moderate climates so they become too warm for their current agricultural production.

The partial destruction of the ozone layer is largely attributed to the use of carbofluorides in various kinds of sprays and other products. The consequence might be to allow the sun's rays to penetrate the earth with greater intensity thereby causing a substantial increase in skin cancer.

The free market does not sufficiently deal with these problems. Business competition may be good for raising the quality of products and lowering prices. Businesses, however, do not compete for consumers on the basis of their use of fossil fuels or carbofluorides. Likewise, regulation may not be so effective because the profits from not complying may be greater than the likely penalties.

For both kinds of pollution, the ideal SOS alternative would be to develop new technologies that are both more profitable and cleaner. The incentive to adopt such technologies would then be the increased profits, rather than competitive or regulatory pressures. Some substitutes have been developed for carbofluorides and for fossil fuels which do have those characteristics. More work on these technologies needs to be done.

**Table 9.9    Global Pollution**

| | GOALS | |
| | Conservative | Liberal |
| ALTERNATIVES | Production and profit. | Clean air. |
| --- | --- | --- |
| **Conservative** <br> Free market. | + | − |
| **Liberal** <br> Regulation. | − | + |
| **Neutral** <br> In between. | 0 | 0 |
| **SOS or Win-Win** <br> Replace fossil fuels and <br> carbo-fluorides. | ++ | ++ |

## Approaches to the Carrying Capacity of the World

Carrying capacity is a phrase that refers to how big a population the world can support given current resources and expertise in how to use those resources.

This problem does not lend itself to conservative versus liberal categories since each group differs within itself on the dimension of optimism and pessimism. The conservative optimists may be more in agreement with the liberal optimists than they are with the conservative pessimists, even though both kinds of conservatives believe in the importance of private enterprise and the marketplace. Likewise, liberal optimists may not agree with liberal pessimists on the policies to be adopted, even though they may agree on the importance of government and public policy in encouraging socially desired behavior.

As a result, the opposing groups are labeled #1 and #2. They both have quality of life as their key goal, but they differ in their perceptions of how various alternatives relate to that goal.

The first group (which tends to be more pessimistic) advocates conservation and population control, which they perceive as having a high score on quality of life. The second group (which tends to be

## Table 9.10 Carrying Capacity of the World

|  | GOALS | |
| --- | --- | --- |
| **ALTERNATIVES** | **Conservative** Quality of life. | **Liberal** Quality of life. |
| **Conservative (#1)** 1. Technology development. 2. Skills upgrading. | + | − |
| **Liberal (#2)** 1. Conservation. 2. Population control. | − | + |
| **Neutral** Some of both. | 0 | 0 |
| **SOS or Win-Win** All of both. | ++ | ++ |

more optimistic) advocates technology development and skills upgrading, which they perceive as having a higher score on quality of life.

The compromise position would be to have some of both alternatives, but not enough conservation and population control to satisfy group #1 and not enough technology development and skills upgrading to satisfy group #2.

The SOS alternative advocates going all out for both the first alternative and the second alternative. That means a four-part program covering conservation, population control, technology development, and skills upgrading.

For conservation, we are especially talking about energy conservation. That could mean developing transportation methods which involve relatively low oil consumption, such as compact cars or electric cars. For population control, one can talk in terms of better technologies, like the new skin implant. More important might be removing the causes of having excess children through relevant public policies such as: (1) more effective social security systems to provide for the elderly, (2) more effective health care to lower the child mortality rate, (3) more legislation to promote opportunities for women to decrease the incentive to have additional children until a male is born, and (4) more higher education opportunities for rural children so that parents will have a stake in limiting the number of children for whom higher education needs to be provided.

On technology development, public policy can provide for tax credits and grants to encourage innovations and especially the adopting of innovations that have already occurred. On skills upgrading, public policy could provide for a 1 percent tax on gross payroll that is completely refunded if the money is used for upgrading the skills of the employees of the businesses. Otherwise, the tax goes into a general fund for supporting on-the-job training and adult education. A refundable tax could also be used to encourage business firms to adopt new technologies.

# Solid and Toxic Waste

## Solid Waste Collection

Conservatives tend to favor privatization in sold waste collection in order to increase individual responsibility and reduce taxes. Liberals tend to favor government collection with recycling in order to increase community responsibility and provide for a cleaner environment.

A compromise is to provide for contracting out by the city government. That is better from a conservative viewpoint than solid waste collection by government employees, but not so good as having each residence or business arrange for solid waste collection. Contracting out is better from a liberal viewpoint than total privatization because the government is in control of who will get the contract and what the contract provisions will be more than if the government tries to regulate the solid waste collectors, but not as much as the government doing the collecting itself.

**Table 9.11  Solid Waste Collection**

| | GOALS | |
|---|---|---|
| **ALTERNATIVES** | **Conservative**<br>1. Individual responsibility.<br>2. Reduce taxes. | **Liberal**<br>1. Community responsibility.<br>2. Clean environment. |
| **Conservative**<br>Privatization. | + | − |
| **Liberal**<br>Government collection with recycling. | − | + |
| **Neutral**<br>Contracting out. | 0 | 0 |
| **SOS or Win-Win**<br>1. Vouchers to reduce<br>    solid waste.<br>2. Contracting out. | ++ | ++ |

A SOS solution would be one that reduces the cost of the contract and provides for an even cleaner environment by preventing the solid waste form coming into existence or needing collection. That can be done by giving homeowners and businesses vouchers to buy various kinds of equipment and services that will reduce the need for solid waste collection. An example would be a voucher for buying a mulcher for one's lawnmower to reduce the need for grass collection. Another example would be a voucher for buying an aluminum-can compactor, which substantially reduces the cost and expense of collecting and recycling tin cans.

Regulated privatization may be more of a SOS alternative than contracting out. The regulation requires private haulers to pick up recyclables. If recycling is purely voluntary, it does not get done so well. The regulation also requires every businesses and household to arrange for hauling of garbage and recyclables. That is a mix of liberal regulation with private enterprise doing the work. The government is in control, but the contracting out is by businesses and households.

## How Far to Go in Toxic Cleanups

The issue here is how far should the cleanup of toxic wastes go. The conservative position is to leave the toxic waste dumps as they are or cover them up in such a way as to decrease the danger without incurring a lot of expenses.

The liberal position is a total cleanup with no toxic waste left. The neutral position is a partial cleanup, until the monetary costs exceed the monetary benefits.

The conservative goal is to reduce business expenses, on which the conservative alternative does well. The liberal goal is to reduce public health risks, on which the liberal alternative does well.

A SOS alternative might be to cleanup until there is no substantial danger. The SOS would allow for government participation in covering the costs from the point where they exceed the benefits up to the point where there is no substantial danger. The government should also be funding research on how to minimize the cost of toxic

**Table 9.12  Toxic Cleanups**

| | GOALS | |
| ALTERNATIVES | Conservative<br>Reduce business expenses. | Liberal<br>Reduce public health risks. |
|---|---|---|
| **Conservative**<br>Leave as is or cover up. | + | – |
| **Liberal**<br>Total cleanup. | – | + |
| **Neutral**<br>Partial cleanup until costs exceed benefits. | 0 | 0 |
| **SOS or Win-Win**<br>Clean up until no substantial danger with government participation. | ++ | ++ |

cleanup by finding ways of recycling the wastes, neutralizing them, or inexpensively covering them up.

That kind of SOS reduces business expenses below the neutral level, while also reducing public health risks below the neutral level. The SOS should therefore exceed the total score of the conservative alternative on the conservative totals, and simultaneously exceed the score of the liberal alternative on the liberal totals.

The Clinton administration is proposing to modify the original liberal position of the Superfund law by substituting a standard like "no health danger" for total cleanup. That means a different degree of cleanup for a residential neighborhood, industrial site, or a wilderness area. It also means that a businesses can locate a factory on a former toxic waste dump without having to restore the dump to a health level fit for a housing development.

## Who Pays for Toxic Cleanups

The issue here is who should pay the cost for cleaning up toxic waste dumps. If the toxic dump was an intentional violation of the law, then there can be criminal prosecution as well. Likewise, if individuals are physically damaged, they can sue for tort damages. The issue here is not criminal or tort liability, but rather allocation of the cleanup costs.

The conservative position is that the government should pay the cost as a public health measure. This is like the conservative position on reducing pollution in general. That position resists levying taxes on the businesses that do the polluting, rather than paying the costs out of general income taxes.

The liberal position is that there should be joint and several liability. That means that the government can go after any or all of the businesses, municipalities, or individuals who are responsible for the toxic waste dump. If the government collects from one firm, then that firm can go after the others to be reimbursed in proportion to their responsibility or whatever the one firm can negotiate.

A neutral position might involve the government going after each firm only for the firm's proportionate share of the costs, not the total costs. The counter-argument is that the firms should have the responsibility for deciding reimbursement among themselves, rather

**Table 9.13 Paying for Toxic Cleanups**

| | GOALS | |
|---|---|---|
| **ALTERNATIVES** | **Conservative** Business expenses. | **Liberal** Clean up toxic waste by wrongdoers. |
| **Conservative** Government responsibility. | + | − |
| **Liberal** Joint and several liability. | − | + |
| **Neutral** Proportionate liability. | 0 | 0 |
| **SOS or Win-Win** Joint and several liability with government participation. | ++ | ++ |

than put the responsibility on the injured plaintiff or the government which represents the community that has been put at risk.

The main conservative goal is to reduce business expense. The mail liberal goal is to clean up toxic waste by business wrongdoers or other wrongdoers. Government responsibility does minimize business expense, but joint and several liability gets the toxic waste cleaned up by wrongdoers.

A SOS alternative might be to provide for joint and several liability, but with the government covering the cost for businesses that have gone bankrupt or disappeared. This reduces business expense better than proportionate liability. It also gets the funding needed to have the toxic waste cleaned up by the wrongdoers under proportionate liability.

The Clinton administration is proposing to modify the original liberal position of the Superfund law by encouraging negotiation and arbitration to determine a proportionate liability for the costs. That approach gives the government the option of developing a combination of joint-several liability, proportionate liability, and government funding for each toxic waste site, depending on the circumstances.

# Wilderness and Species Preservation

### Lumbering Regulation

The conservative position on lumbering is to leave it to the marketplace, meaning that each lumbering company should decide for itself how much cutting it wants to do in a given year. The liberal position is to prohibit lumbering of certain forests in order to preserve their natural state and the wildlife. A compromise position is to allow lumbering companies more unrestrained decision making than the liberals advocate, but less than the conservatives advocate.

The conservatives are especially interested in having the lumber industry be profitable. The liberals are especially interested in saving some forests from destruction, including the preservation of wildlife.

The SOS object is thus to enable lumbering to be both profitable and at the same time provide for adequate conservation. That can be

**Table 9.14 Lumbering**

| | GOALS | |
|---|---|---|
| | **Conservative**<br>Lumber profits. | **Liberal**<br>1. Save endangered<br>species.<br>2. Save wild recreation. |
| **ALTERNATIVES** | | |
| **Conservative**<br>Marketplace. | + | − |
| **Liberal**<br>Prohibit lumbering. | − | + |
| **Neutral**<br>Percentage harvesting. | 0 | 0 |
| **SOS or Win-Win**<br>1. Sanctuary.<br>2. Retraining. | ++ | ++ |

done to some extent by way of systematic percentage harvesting of forests. Such a system involves cutting maybe 20 percent of the forest each year. Doing so allows the forest to remain and regrow indefinitely. This can keep profits coming in the future, as contrasted to clearcutting which may be highly profitable in the first year, but no profits for a long time thereafter.

A SOS alternative might also provide for wildlife sanctuaries where endangered species can be brought to live without the destructiveness of lumbering. The SOS alternative might also involve some retraining of lumbering workers with regard to other more employable skills if lumber workers are being reduced as a result of new lumbering technologies, the diminishing of forests, and new technologies to replace lumber with other materials.

## Policy toward Hunting

On the matter of hunting animals, conservatives are in favor of virtually unlimited hunting, although excluding the shooting of pets or livestock.

**Table 9.15 Hunting**

| | GOALS | |
|---|---|---|
| **ALTERNATIVES** | **Conservative**<br>1. Macho interaction.<br>2. Profits. | **Liberal**<br>Save animals. |
| **Conservative**<br>Unlimited hunting. | + | − |
| **Liberal**<br>No hunting. | − | + |
| **Neutral**<br>Some hunting. | 0 | 0 |
| **SOS or Win-Win**<br>Hunting with<br>conservation and safety. | ++ | ++ |

Liberals want virtually no hunting of wild animals, although they are willing to tolerate the killing of livestock for food.

A compromise position might be some hunting but with limitations as to time, place, and quantity, not necessarily related to conservation.

The conservative goal is to preserve the macho interaction of hunting and the commercial profits. The liberal goal is to save the animals.

A super-optimum solution might be hunting with conservation and safety rules. The pro-hunters should endorse the conservation rules since they preserve game for future hunting. The anti-hunters should consider the conservation rules as saving some animals who otherwise would be hunted and destroyed. Pro-hunters should welcome safety rules that keep them from getting shot. Anti-hunters should also welcome safety rules, since they presumably value the lives of human beings and not just animals.

A new development in hunting is the raising of game animals on game farms for hunting purposes. This may be needed because of the reduction in wild animals. The wild animals, though, may have a better quality of life than animals kept in captivity. Anti-hunters may be even more opposed to raising game animals since shooting them comes closer to shooting pets, which is not tolerated in our society, but it also comes close to shooting or killing livestock, which is tolerated. This new development thus does not alleviate or worsen the policy issue.

## Releasing Wolves in the West

The problem here is that saving endangered species sometimes involves protecting predator animals like wolves or hawks that prey on livestock and sometimes pets.

The conservative position is to allow these animals to be killed off and not preserved. The liberal position is to prohibit killing them, except in self-defense or in defense of livestock, and to release such animals into national parks and wilderness areas.

A neutral position is to only release a small quantity and to keep the quantity down by thinning out the predatory animals through encouraging hunting of them when necessary.

The conservative goal is to preserve livestock and pets. The liberal goal is to preserve natural wilderness and to thin the surplus

**Table 9.16  Releasing Wolves**

| | GOALS | |
| | Conservative<br>Preserving livestock. | Liberal<br>1. Preserving wilderness.<br>2. Thin deer. |
| **ALTERNATIVES** | | |
| **Conservative**<br>No releasing. | + | − |
| **Liberal**<br>Have releasing. | − | + |
| **Neutral**<br>Limited releasing. | 0 | 0 |
| **SOS or Win-Win**<br>1. Limited releasing.<br>2. Compensation for<br>losses to property<br>owners. | ++ | ++ |

population of deer or other animals. The predatory animals may also be relevant to preserving ecological balance.

A SOS solution might involve limited release combined with compensation for losses to property owners and compensation to cover traps or other devices on ranches to keep the predators off ranch property. That kind of solution preserves some livestock and compensates for the livestock that cannot be preserved, while simultaneously allowing for wilderness-environment protection.

# Special Types of Environmental Protection or Conservation

### SOS Analysis on Smoking Policy

Regulation can include: (1) no smoking in airplanes and other public places, (2) no advertising on TV or radio, and (3) prohibitions on sales to minors at stores or vending machines.

Information can include: (1) warnings on cigarette packages and on ads, (2) requiring equal time for anti-smoking information on

**Table 9.17  Smoking Policy**

|  | GOALS | |
| --- | --- | --- |
| **ALTERNATIVES** | **Conservative**<br>Preserve free market. | **Liberal**<br>Reduce smoking. |
| **Conservative**<br>No government<br>interference. | + | – |
| **Liberal**<br>Regulation. | – | + |
| **Neutral**<br>Information. | 0 | 0 |
| **SOS or Win-Win**<br>1. Regulation.<br>2. Information<br>3. Incentives. | ++ | ++ |

television or radio, and (3) encouraging anti-smoking learning modules in preschool, elementary, and high school.

Incentives can include: (1) funding to find a new type of cigarette that would satisfy, but contains no nicotine or tars, (2) funding under health care programs to enable smokers to stop smoking, and (3) funding to cover the educational costs of media and schools.

Conservatives are becoming more supportive of approaches to reducing smoking because smoking: (1) generates tremendous societal health care costs, (2) causes non-smokers to be more likely to get cancer or other diseases, (3) wastes a lot of money that could be spent on other more useful products, (4) reduces productivity, increases absenteeism, and lessens the quality of workplaces.

Arguments designed to win over liberals include: (1) cigarettes provide tax money, but the societal costs outweigh the revenue, and taxes could be raised elsewhere, (2) cigarettes kill people and thereby save the government their social security payments, but that is an argument for encouraging premature cancer, heart disease, diabetes, and other aging killers, and (3) cigarette regulation interferes with a right to privacy, but harm is done to others, and there is no prohibition on private smoking.

## A SOS Perspective on Flood Control

Table 9.18 is prompted by the 1993 floods mainly in the upper Mississippi and Missouri rivers. Some of the ideas are applicable to other natural disasters.

The conservative position emphasizes a minimum of government involvement in order to keep down the heavy tax burden that might be incurred. The liberal position emphasizes expensive flood control and insurance by the government in order to save lives, injuries, and disruption to people who are not adequately covered by savings and insurance.

An additional goal of the relatively neutral might be the reduction of property damage. The property damaged in floods and other natural disasters tends to be in relatively low-income areas. High-income property owners are less likely to locate in high-risk areas.

**Table 9.18  Flood Control**

|  | GOALS | |
| --- | --- | --- |
| **ALTERNATIVES** | **Conservative**<br>Reduce tax. | **Liberal**<br>Save lives and injuries. |
| **Conservative**<br>Minimum of government<br>involvement. | + | − |
| **Liberal**<br>Prevent flood damage and<br>compensate. | − | + |
| **Neutral**<br>In between. | 0 | 0 |
| **SOS or Win-Win**<br>Channel flood water to<br>where needed. | ++ | ++ |

They are also more likely to be covered by savings and insurance.

A SOS solution should be capable of reducing the tax burden at least in the long run and also saving lives, injuries, and disruption. Perhaps a SOS solution might be a system of reservoirs and pipelines to channel floodwaters to areas needing more water.

That type of solution could reduce the long-run tax burden by enabling land further west to become much more productive. Doing so would add to the national income and increase tax revenue without raising tax rates. The SOS solution could also save tax costs that might otherwise be spent on repairing the damage from such floods. At the same time, the SOS would save lives, injuries, and disruption.

A key question is the matter of economic feasibility. One form that question takes is whether the cost of the system of reservoirs and pipelines would be more than offset by the increased GNP, the increased tax base, and the saving of flood-related costs. If the offset is greater, then this is probably a SOS solution.

Another form the feasibility question takes is, can the federal government afford the cost of such a flood control system? The answers are: (1) yes, in comparison to the willingness of the private sector to invest in such a system that may not pay off for a while; (2) yes, in recognition of the fact that the private sector cannot sell water to western farmers, and it does not benefit directly enough from the increased GNP the way the nation as a whole does; (3) yes, in terms of the political feasibility if the initial cost is more than offset by the benefits mentioned above; and (4) yes, in terms of technological feasibility if the system if not much more technologically difficult than the system of natural gas pipelines from the Southwest to the Midwest, or the aqueducts to Rome from distant provinces.

# Chapter 10

## Housing

### Housing for the Poor

#### Alternative Policies for Providing Housing for the Poor

In light of the scores of the policies on the goals, the condominium arrangement seems best for existing government-owned public housing. That policy is, however, resisted partly because the present public-housing management does not want to become the employees of the tenants.

In light of the scores of the policies on the goals, the rent supplements seem best for providing housing for the poor outside of government-owned public housing projects. That policy is, however, resisted partly because it means appropriating new federal funds.

The program of home ownership for the poor might have been effectively administered if the intermediaries were HUD employees who have no commission incentive to de-emphasize maintenance costs or to bribe property assessors as part of repeated foreclosure schemes with the federal government covering the mortgages.

One could add the policy of doing nothing to provide housing for the poor. Such a policy at first glance looks good with regard to the burden on the taxpayer. It could, however, result in unacceptable slum living conditions that could be an even greater burden on the taxpayer than helping to provide affordable housing.

**Table 10.1 (Old) Housing for the Poor**

| | GOALS | |
|---|---|---|
| | **Conservative** | **Liberal** |
| | 1. Low burden on taxpayer: building cost, maintenance cost. | Affordable housing for the poor. |
| | 2. Incentive for work and law compliance. | |
| **ALTERNATIVES** | 3. Stimulate housing development. | |
| **Conservative** | | |
| 1. Private ownership with government rent subsidies. | | |
| 2. Government ownership with condo ownership. | + | − |
| 3. Private ownership with government purchase subsidies and private sector intermediaries. | | |
| **Liberal** | | |
| 1. Rent control. | | |
| 2. Government owned high-rise housing. | − | + |
| 3. Government owned low-rise housing. | | |
| **Neutral** | | |
| Likely to be effectively administered. | 0 | 0 |
| **SOS or Win-Win** | | |
| See text. | ++ | ++ |

## Evaluating Policies for Providing Housing for the Poor

The former liberal alternative of large-scale public housing is being abandoned by liberals because of its adverse relations to goals that liberals formerly thought benefitted from large-scale public housing.

Rent supplements involve adding to the rent that a tenant pays so as to satisfy the landlord's need for a reasonable rent without exceeding the tenant's ability to pay.

**Table 10.2 (New) Housing for the Poor**

| | GOALS | |
|---|---|---|
| **ALTERNATIVES** | **Conservative**<br>Stimulate housing<br>development. | **Liberal**<br>1. Decent housing for the<br>    poor.<br>2. Equity: race/class. |
| **Conservative**<br>Marketplace. | + | – |
| **Liberal**<br>Large scale public<br>housing. | – | + |
| **Neutral**<br>1. Low rise public<br>    housing.<br>2. Condos.<br>3. Home ownership. | 0 | 0 |
| **SOS or Win-Win**<br>1. Rent supplement.<br>2. Skills upgrade. | ++ | ++ |

Skills upgrading in this context refers to improving the employ-ability of the poor and the homeless so they can afford to pay a reasonable rent.

See Table 10.3 entitled "(Simple) Housing for the Poor" for a more recent and simplified perspective on the problem, along with more detailed notes.

## A SOS Analysis of Housing for the Poor

The conservative approach to housing for the poor is to leave it up to the marketplace. The liberal approach is to provide for public housing that is owned or subsidized by the government and rented to low-income people at rents below the market level. The neutral position is to budget more for public housing than conservatives would, but less than liberals would.

Public housing when it was first developed in the 1930s meant large projects owned by the government. As of the 1960s, liberals turned against such projects because they became unpleasant places in which to live given the congestion of so many poor people and juveniles in a small area. The major modifications involved requiring future public housing to be low-rise rather than high-rise and also to give the tenants more control over the management process.

Conservatives, in the context of housing for the poor, are interested in keeping tax expenditures down and in aiding private sector housing. The liberal goal is decent housing for the poor. The marketplace may be able to provide some housing for the poor, but not above a minimum level of decency and quality.

The SOS alternative might be rent supplements or vouchers. They involve, for example, a low-income recipient paying $300 toward a $400 apartment and the government providing a $100 voucher to make up the difference. The voucher can only be used for private sector housing. That system involves less tax expenditures than traditional public housing, and it does put money into the private sector marketplace. It can also provide better quality housing than public housing.

Along with rent supplements can go a program for upgrading the skills of recipients. They can then increase their incomes and eventually no longer need the rent supplements. The skills upgrading

**Table 10.3  (Simple) Housing for the Poor**

|  | GOALS | |
|---|---|---|
| **ALTERNATIVES** | **Conservative**<br>1. Reduce taxes.<br>2. Aid private sector<br>housing. | **Liberal**<br>Decent housing for the<br>poor. |
| **Conservative**<br>Marketplace. | + | − |
| **Liberal**<br>Modified public housing. | − | + |
| **Neutral**<br>In between. | 0 | 0 |
| **SOS or Win-Win**<br>1. Rent supplements.<br>2. Skills upgrading. | ++ | ++ |

may be especially important for the homeless who may have virtually no incomes.

The voucher system also has the extra benefit of facilitating economic class integration. A requirement in using the vouchers might be that one has to use them in neighborhoods that are above the concentrated poverty level. Doing so facilitates school integration in terms of low-income children going to school with middle-class children. It also stimulates ambition on the part of the parents more so than living in public housing.

## Sweep Searches at Public Housing

The police have been conducting sweep searches of apartments in public housing projects in Chicago. Such a search involves searching all or random apartments for drugs, guns, and other incriminating evidence. The searches have been declared unconstitutional.

The liberal position (as endorsed by the federal courts) is that the Constitution allows police searches only when there is probable cause or a substantial probability of finding incriminating evidence in the apartment. The probable cause standard should be applied to each individual apartment. It should also be used when a search warrant is issued.

The conservative position (as endorsed by the police and the public housing authority) is that the searches should be allowed since they do uncover some drugs and guns, and they do deter some drugs and guns in the apartments.

The liberal goal is privacy for the numerous apartment dwellers who do not have incriminating evidence in their apartments. The conservative goal is to reduce the presence of guns and drugs in the public housing projects.

The object of a SOS alternative is to simultaneously reduce guns and drugs more than sweep searches do, and to preserve privacy more than the probable-cause standard does. An approach to doing that might involve security guards at the entrance to each public housing project making use of metal detectors to detect guns, and dog sniffing to detect drugs.

The metal detectors may find and deter more guns than the sweep searches. It is easier to hide a gun from a hurried occasional search than it is to hide a gun from a daily metal-detector. It may also be more difficult to hide drugs from daily dog-sniffing than from a hurried occasional search.

The approach of metal detectors and dog sniffing at the entrance also provides more privacy than having a lot of probable cause searches. The SOS proposal does not in itself involve any searches of apartments, although it could be supplemented with legal searches based on probable cause.

When the federal court declared the sweep searches unconstitutional, President Clinton announced that the Justice Department and HUD would develop a search policy for nationwide public housing that would be both constitutional and effective. That is a good example of super-optimum thinking, as contrasted to a compromise that might seek to relax probable cause standards and thereby allow a lot of apartments to be searched, but not all of them. The result would be less effective than sweep searches, and more invasions of privacy than probable cause.

**Table 10.4  Searches at Public Housing**

|  | GOALS | |
| --- | --- | --- |
| | **Conservative** | **Liberal** |
| | Effectively reduce guns | Privacy. |
| **ALTERNATIVES** | and drugs. | |
| **Conservative** <br> All apartments. | + | − |
| **Liberal** <br> Probable cause. | − | + |
| **Neutral** <br> Relax standards. | 0 | 0 |
| **SOS or Win-Win** <br> 1. Metal detectors. <br> 2. Dog sniffing. | ++ | ++ |

# Special Categories of People Needing Housing

## Policy toward the Homeless

The problem of homelessness is different from the problem of housing for the poor. The latter problem usually involves people who have a place to live, but the housing may be beneath a minimum threshold of quality in terms of the socio-physical environment and unnecessarily expensive. The homeless by definition have no home at all, but instead sleep in parks, alleys, boxes, or whatever can be found.

The conservative position is to provide emergency aid to keep people from freezing to death, but otherwise largely a hands-off position to deter homelessness and to decrease the tax burden.

The liberal position is to provide housing in the form of apartments, or at least dormitory facilities, in order to improve the quality of life of the homeless.

A compromise position is to treat most of the homeless as being addicts, alcoholics, or mentally ill. This position emphasizes therapy as a solution.

**Table 10.5 Homeless**

| | GOALS | |
| --- | --- | --- |
| ALTERNATIVES | **Conservative**<br>1. Deter homelessness.<br>2. Reduce taxes. | **Liberal**<br>Quality of life. |
| **Conservative**<br>1. Marketplace.<br>2. Emergency aid. | + | − |
| **Liberal**<br>Housing apartments. | − | + |
| **Neutral**<br>Therapy. | 0 | 0 |
| **SOS or Win-Win**<br>1. Training.<br>2. Jobs. | ++ | ++ |

A super-optimum solution might be to emphasize training and job opportunities. Doing so can lead to increased incomes that can cover at least part of the cost of livable housing. Doing so can also lessen mental and addiction problems. In addition, it can result in adding to the GNP, the paying of taxes, and being better role models.

Training and jobs cost money but so does housing, therapy, and emergency aid. The important thing is that such an approach may have a substantial economic payoff that can more than justify the societal investment in the training and jobs.

## Students as Tenants

There are many issues that are argued between landlords in a university community and student tenants. One is how to handle security deposits.

The liberal position is that the deposits should be placed in an escrow fund. The fund cannot be used for anything except to return the deposit when the apartment is vacated without damage, or to fully or partially retain the deposit if the apartment is damaged. The money in the fund should collect interest at the average savings account rate in the community.

The conservative position is no escrow fund and no interest on security deposits. A compromise position might provide that half the deposit goes into an escrow fund, with interest accumulating at a rate below the market rate.

The conservative position adds to the landlord's profits especially if the deposits can be invested with a return to the landlord, or never repaid if the landlord goes bankrupt or ceases to be the landlord. The liberal position is oriented toward increasing the rights of the tenant to get back the deposit and with interest. Neither position is relevant to university income.

A super-optimum solution might be for the university to contract out its dormitories to the highest bidding landlords in an auction arrangement. The contract would specify such tenant rights as an escrow fund with interest.

**Table 10.6 Students as Tenants**

| ALTERNATIVES | GOALS | |
| --- | --- | --- |
| | Conservative<br>Landlord profits. | Liberal<br>Tenant rights. |
| **Conservative**<br>1. No escrow fund.<br>2. No interest on security<br>deposits. | + | − |
| **Liberal**<br>1. Escrow fund.<br>2. Interest. | − | + |
| **Neutral**<br>1. Partial escrow.<br>2. Low interest. | 0 | 0 |
| **SOS or Win-Win**<br>Contracting out. | ++ | ++ |

The arrangement might provide that the landlords rent the dormitories from the university at about 60 percent of what the students are paying, but the landlords absorb all the expenses. The university should thereby come out ahead in terms of net income.

The landlords rent to the students at about 90 percent of what the students were formerly paying to the university. The landlords are required to meet various quality specifications. Otherwise, the lease is not renewed by the university. This enables students to come out ahead of the previous situation.

The landlords should be able to make a profit if they operate efficiently. The exact percentages may have to be negotiated so as to enable all three groups to come out ahead of the previous situation with a new source of profits for landlords, lower rents for students, and more income for the university. This assumes that the private profit motive associated with well managed competitive housing can be more efficient and profitable than near-monopolistic state-run housing.

This is a good illustration of where contracting out may make more sense than selling out since the state or university retains the power to refuse to renew if the contract is violated. It is also mutually more profitable than a compromise of a mixed system of some purely state-run dormitories and some purely private housing.

The illustration can be extended to include other kinds of contracting out by the government, such as possibly the educational program as well as the housing program. It does not apply to contracting out public housing. There the problem is too many poor people concentrated in one place. A housing voucher system makes more sense for that problem to widely disperse poor people into middle class neighborhoods, but we do not want to widely disperse university students.

# Chapter 11

---

# Transportation and Communication

## Bicycles versus Cars

### The Problem of Collisions between Bicycles and Cars

The benefits of increasing safety include reducing injuries, reducing traffic disruption, and reducing ambulance costs. The components of the cost variable include equipment costs and enforcement costs, and interference costs. Positive and negative

**Table 11.1 Collisions between Bicycles and Cars**

| | GOALS | |
| --- | --- | --- |
| | **Conservative**<br>Decrease cost. | **Liberal**<br>1. Increase safety. |
| **ALTERNATIVES** | | 2. Equity. |
| **Conservative**<br>1. Do nothing.<br>2. No night bikes.<br>3. Buy reflectors.<br>4. Subsidize manufacturer. | + | − |
| **Liberal**<br>1. Reflectors.<br>2. Lights.<br>3. Free reflectors.<br>4. Require manufacturers. | − | + |
| **Neutral** | 0 | 0 |
| **SOS or Win-Win**<br>See text. | ++ | ++ |

values are now shown on those goals because they are subgoals of the main goals of safety and cost, although values could be shown if one wants further details.

Values on the equity goal are only shown and added for comparing free reflectors with buying reflectors since that is where the equity goal is mainly involved. Likewise, values on the feasibility goals are only shown for prohibiting bicycles at night since that alternative is not politically or administratively feasible.

## Bicycles versus Cars

The transportation problem of bicycles versus cars especially occurs in developing nations that have relied heavily on bicycle transportation and that are now having an upsurge in accidents as a result of the increase in automobiles. That is true of the big cities in China like Beijing.

Doing nothing or prohibiting night biking may involve no tax cost in terms of a government subsidy. There may, however, be substantial

**Table 11.2 (Simple) Bicycles versus Cars**

| | GOALS | |
|---|---|---|
| ALTERNATIVES | Conservative<br>1. Decrease cost.<br>2. Increase business. | Liberal<br>Safety. |
| **Conservative**<br>1. Do nothing.<br>2. Prohibit night biking. | + | − |
| **Liberal**<br>1. Free reflectors.<br>2. Required reflectors. | − | + |
| **Neutral**<br>1. Partial free reflectors.<br>2. Partially subsidized<br>   reflectors. | 0 | 0 |
| **SOS or Win-Win**<br>Reflecting paint. | ++ | ++ |

costs from injuries, traffic disruption, and ambulance costs if doing nothing means increasing accidents. Prohibiting night biking may not be politically or administratively feasible. It may also be quite expensive to enforce.

Free reflectors are less expensive to the government than free battery-operated lights. They are, however, more expensive than requiring bikers to buy their own reflectors. Required reflectors, in this context, refers to requiring manufacturers to provide reflectors at their own expense.

Partially free reflectors means that the bikers and the government would each pay part of the cost. Partially subsidized reflectors means that the manufacturers and the government would each pay part of the cost.

Requiring reflecting paint in the manufacturing of future bicycles involves no extra taxpayer cost. It involves no extra business cost if the reflecting paint costs about the same as regular paint. It does add to the safety since the whole bicycle becomes a reflector, and is less likely to be hit by a car or to cause a car to swerve at the last minute to avoid the bicycle.

## Manila Commuting Problem

The SOS refers partly to stimulating job opportunities in the suburbs so as to reduce the commuter congestion to the central city.

The SOS also refers partly to developing regional cities or cities that are in relatively rural areas to provide employment opportunities that would decrease the movement from rural areas to the big cities.

The SOS further refers to developing freer immigration across countries in order to facilitate ambitious people finding job opportunities.

## Table 11.3 Commuter

| ALTERNATIVES | GOALS | |
|---|---|---|
| | **Conservative**<br>Decrease taxes. | **Liberal**<br>Decrease time<br>commuting. |
| **Conservative**<br>As is. | + | − |
| **Liberal**<br>Mass transit. | − | + |
| **Neutral**<br>Hodge podge with more<br>jeepneys and buses. | 0 | 0 |
| **SOS or Win-Win**<br>Suburbs, regional cities,<br>overseas, and other<br>employment centers. | ++ | ++ |

## Table 11.4 Federal Aviation Administration

| ALTERNATIVES | GOALS | |
|---|---|---|
| | **Conservative**<br>Decrease airline costs. | **Liberal**<br>Safety. |
| **Conservative**<br>1. Reduce labor cost.<br>2. Reduce equipment cost. | + | − |
| **Liberal**<br>1. Pay high labor cost.<br>2. Pay high equipment<br>   cost. | − | + |
| **Neutral**<br>In between. | 0 | 0 |
| **SOS or Win-Win**<br>1. No-wage benefits.<br>2. Subsidy for high safety<br>   and low cost systems. | ++ | ++ |

# Federal Aviation Administration Policy

The conservative goal is to aid airline and airport management to make a profit. The liberal goal is higher wages for the workers while preserving aviation safety.

The conservative alternative of reducing labor and equipment costs could jeopardize safety by laying off needed traffic controllers. The liberal alternative of paying a high labor bill and equipment bill lessens airline profits although it may increase airline safety.

The SOS alternative is to provide non-wage benefits to the workers, such as more breaks and time off given the stressful nature of air traffic control. The SOS alternative might also involve well-placed subsidies to encourage the development and diffusion of air traffic control systems that score high on safety but low on cost.

That is an example of what is sometimes referred to as quality technology. Such technology increases productivity but simultaneously provides a better quality workplace, environment, and consumer protection.

# Communications Industry

### A SOS Perspective on the Developing Communications Industry

Table 11.5 relates to the mergers that are under way involving companies that deal with telephones, cable television, electricity, movies, and other companies that are relevant to what is sometimes referred to as the worldwide communications highway.

The problem is how to get the benefits from economies of scale and from merging different kinds of technologies without having the drawbacks that are associated with monopolistic big business.

The conservative position in dealing with telephones, cable television, and electricity has been tolerant of monopoly and tolerant of prohibiting or strictly regulating new entrants. This is good for the profits of existing firms at least in the short run.

The traditional liberal position has advocated government

ownership of telephone and electric companies, along with price control and equitable access to protect consumers.

The compromise position is limited entry. That includes allowing competition on long-distance telephoning but not requiring licensing of local telephone or electric lines to competing companies. The compromise position may advocate competition between domestic phone companies or electric companies, but not allowing foreign companies to operate in the American telephone or electricity markets.

The SOS position is free entry assuming safety and public health standards are met. It also includes seed money for new and existing firms to be more competitive, especially internationally competitive.

That kind of SOS emphasis on competition should be good for consumers and also good for businesses that would like to enter into these otherwise closed markets. It can also be good for existing firms by stimulating them to become more efficient and more profitable. The profit per firm may or may not go up, but the profit for the industry should go up substantially as a result of better servicing of more consumers in the domestic and international markets.

**Table 11.5  Communications Industry**

|  | GOALS | |
|---|---|---|
|  | **Conservative**<br>Profits for existing firms. | **Liberal**<br>1. Lower prices.<br>2. Better products for |
| **ALTERNATIVES** |  | consumers. |
| **Conservative**<br>1. Regulation of entry.<br>2. Toleration monopoly. | + | − |
| **Liberal**<br>1. Government<br>  ownership.<br>2. Price control. | − | + |
| **Neutral**<br>Limited entry. | 0 | 0 |
| **SOS or Win-Win**<br>1. Free entry.<br>2. Seed money. | ++ | ++ |

## Funding NEA and PBS

The issue here relates to funding the National Endowment for the Arts (NEA) and the Public Broadcasting System (PBS). Conservatives would like to abolish both government agencies, supposedly to save taxes, but partly to reduce the liberalism that is associated with both agencies.

Liberals would like to retain both agencies to promote art activities and public interest broadcasting in America. A compromise would be to retain both agencies but substantially cut their budgets and encourage them to rely more on private sector contributions, or retain one but not the other.

A SOS solution might be to adopt a variation on the fairness doctrine for the NEA and PBS. That doctrine (as formerly applied to private-sector radio) required some balance between liberal and conservative commentary. The NEA and PBS enabling acts could be amended to provide that at least 20 percent of the expenditures should go toward inspiring widely accepted values that relate to such matters

**Table 11.6 NEA and PBS**

| | GOALS | |
|---|---|---|
| | **Conservative** 1. Save taxes. 2. Reduce liberalism. | **Liberal** 1. Promote art. 2. Promote public interest broadcasting. |
| **ALTERNATIVES** | | |
| **Conservative** 1. Abolish NEA. 2. Abolish PBS. | + | − |
| **Liberal** Retain both. | − | + |
| **Neutral** Cut budgets or retain one. | 0 | 0 |
| **SOS or Win-Win** 1. Fairness doctrine. 2. Expand both conservative and liberal art and broadcasting. | ++ | ++ |

as free speech, merit treatment, due process, the work ethic, patrio-
tism, and education. Doing so should please both conservatives and
liberals.

Additional appropriations could be provided to include an
expansion of activities relating to inspiring such values. Of the 20
percent, half the funding could relate to inspiring values that
conservatives especially endorse and half to values more associated
with liberals. The object is to provide more inspiration and more
balance in both the NEA and PBS.

# Section B

# Better Science Policy:
# Physical and Biological

# Chapter 12

---

# Energy

## Energy Sources

### Raw Data for Choosing Energy Policies

One should note that each policy has sub-policies:

1. Nuclear can be divided into uranium (the most common form), plutonium, and hydrogen.
2. Oil can be divided into known deposits and unknown deposits.
3. Coal can be divided into high-polluting (the most common form) and low-polluting.
4. Synthetic fuels can be divided into natural (like oil shale) and artificial (like garbage).
5. Solar can be divided into small-scale and large-scale.

One should note the big drawback for each energy source:

1. Nuclear lacks sufficient safety, especially nuclear wastes.
2. Oil lacks long-term value.
3. Coal is bad on pollution.
4. Synthetic fuels have high ongoing costs.
5. Solar has high start-up costs for large-scale operations.

The choices can be best viewed in terms of three tracks:

1.  Oil is best on the short-term track.
2.  Coal and synthetic fuels make the most sense on the intermediate track, with a need for developing more economic synthetic fuels.
3.  Solar and nuclear make the most sense on the long-term track, but there is a need for developing safer nuclear energy and for research on implementing large-scale solar energy.

The sequential combination of the SOS alternative refers to emphasizing oil until it is used up, then emphasizing coal until it is used up, and then emphasizing nuclear and solar energy.

A better approach might be well-placed subsidies to bring about safer nuclear energy, and more massive solar energy as soon as possible. Safer nuclear energy means safer power plants, and nuclear waste disposal with traditional uranium nuclear energy. Safer nuclear energy may also mean developing hydrogen nuclear energy that is less likely to involve radioactivity problems.

**Table 12.1 Energy Policies**

| | GOALS | |
| --- | --- | --- |
| **ALTERNATIVES** | **Conservative**<br>1. Cost.<br>2. How soon available. | **Liberal**<br>1. Long-term value.<br>2. Safety. |
| **Conservative**<br>1. Nuclear.<br>2. Oil. | + | − |
| **Liberal**<br>1. Synthetic fuels.<br>2. Solar. | − | + |
| **Neutral**<br>Coal. | 0 | 0 |
| **SOS or Win-Win**<br>1. Sequential combination.<br>2. Well-placed subsidies. | ++ | ++ |

Massive solar energy means subsidizing the development of such technologies as an economically feasible microwave in the sky to disperse solar energy across the world through concentrated laser beams. It may also mean developing better energy storage batteries and capabilities for storing solar energy for use at night, on cloudy days, and at peak usage periods.

## Evaluating Energy Sources

Support for the nuclear industry and the oil industry has traditionally come more from conservative interests than liberal interests, especially in the United States. The opposite is true of solar energy and synthetic fuels, especially since the Carter administration.

Nuclear and oil do better on present business profits and tax costs because they are currently available, whereas solar energy and synthetic fuels would require substantial implementation costs probably by both business and government.

**Table 12.2 Energy Sources**

| | GOALS | |
|---|---|---|
| **ALTERNATIVES** | **Conservative**<br>1. Increase business profits.<br>2. Decrease tax costs. | **Liberal**<br>1. Increase consumers.<br>2. Increase environment.<br>3. International relations. |
| **Conservative**<br>1. Nuclear.<br>2. Oil. | + | − |
| **Liberal**<br>1. Solar.<br>2. Synthetic fuels. | − | + |
| **Neutral**<br>1. Coal.<br>2. Mixture. | 0 | 0 |
| **SOS or Win-Win**<br>1. Safe nuclear.<br>2. Massive solar. | ++ | ++ |

In the long run, solar and synthetic fuels might be better for environmental safety and cleanliness than nuclear or oil, and less expensive. They would also be less expensive than oil when oil becomes more scarce.

## A Possible Deactivation SOS Solution to the Energy Problem

Perhaps the major problem associated with nuclear energy is what to do with the radioactive waste. The possibility of damage from leakage of nuclear wastes may be greater than the possibility of a nuclear reactor exploding or having some other kind of major accident. Even if the nuclear waste problem is not more serious, it is still a big obstacle to safe nuclear energy.

The conservative approach has been to endorse nuclear energy, including the approaches to storing nuclear waste developed by the nuclear industry. Conservatives have traditionally defended the power companies from being attacked by reformers and skeptics. Lately, many conservatives have moved away from the power companies because of monopolistic pricing that can be detrimental to business development.

**Table 12.3 Deactivation of Energy**

| | GOALS | |
| --- | --- | --- |
| **ALTERNATIVES** | **Conservative** Cheap energy. | **Liberal** Safe energy. |
| **Conservative** Nuclear. | + | − |
| **Liberal** Solar. | − | + |
| **Neutral** 1. Both. 2. Conservation. 3. Recycling. | 0 | 0 |
| **SOS or Win-Win** Deactivation if physically and economically possible. | ++ | ++ |

Liberals tend to be highly distrustful of the idea of safe nuclear energy. They therefore tend to advocate solar energy and other non-nuclear, non-fossil fuels. The neutral position might support exploring both safe nuclear energy and large-scale solar energy along with conservation and recycling to save on existing energy sources.

A SOS solution to the nuclear waste problem should be capable of providing cheap energy to satisfy conservatives and safe energy to satisfy liberals. A proposed SOS solution that might be capable of doing that is to accelerate the deactivation of nuclear waste to a matter of years or months, rather than centuries. There is a need for subsidizing research to determine if such a solution is physically and economically possible. This is in contrast to the idea of storing nuclear waste. Storing may be more expensive and less safe than the deactivation idea, although storage can be considered a temporary solution until deactivation is developed.

# Energy Conservation

## Energy Conservation and Super-Optimizing

On the matter of energy conservation, conservatives tend to have a shorter time horizon than liberals. They are more willing to consume oil, coal, and other resources with less concern for saving for the future.

Conservatives may overemphasize present business profits to the detriment of future consumers. Liberals, however, may overemphasize future consumers to the detriment of present income.

A SOS alternative might emphasize new energy sources in order to increase present business profits while still providing for future energy consumers. Safe nuclear energy (such as hydrogen energy) might be such an energy source. It could provide manufacturing firms with less expensive energy. At the same time, hydrogen energy is capable of being available as long as water is available from which hydrogen can be extracted. Likewise, massive solar energy (by way of a microwave space platform with laser beams covering the earth) could provide low-cost energy once the system is in place, and such energy could last forever.

**Table 12.4 Energy Conservation**

|  | GOALS | |
| --- | --- | --- |
| **ALTERNATIVES** | **Conservative**<br>Business profits now. | **Liberal**<br>Future consumers. |
| **Conservative**<br>Oil now. | + | − |
| **Liberal**<br>Conserve for future. | − | + |
| **Neutral**<br>In between. | 0 | 0 |
| **SOS or Win-Win**<br>New energy sources. | ++ | ++ |

Conservation makes sense if it means not wasting resources or other things of value. It may not make sense if it means unnecessarily reducing non-wasteful consumption. An overemphasis on conservation can decrease the incentive to find new energy sources. On the other hand, conservation may help provide backup resources while new energy sources are being developed. The bottom line is probably that conservation versus consumption in the realm of energy is a partial distraction from the more important alternative of developing new energy sources that are more profitable, more lasting, and also cleaner.

New energy sources will not increase business profits as of today. They may do so within the present generation if seed money is made available by the government for faster technological development and diffusion. A key factor holding back that kind of investment is the fact that the present oil availability has not reached a critical point.

**Raising the MPG Standards**

The federal government is contemplating an increase in the average miles per gallon for each auto maker from the current 27.5 mpg to 40 mpg. The conservative position prefers retaining the present mpg or lowering it. The liberal position wants to go 40 mpg.

A compromise would be somewhere in the middle. The mpg standards are averages per auto maker, not minimums.

A low mpg scores well on the conservative goal of avoiding disruption of the profits of auto makers, but not so well on the liberal goal of low pollution. A high mpg does better on low pollution, but would require new engineering by auto makers. This is a classic tradeoff situation that usually leads to a middling compromise.

A SOS alternative might be for the government to subsidize the development of high mpg autos that can be made even less expensively than present autos. That might be the case with autos that are run by batteries, steam engines, hydrogen fuel, solar energy, or other alternatives to the internal combustion engine. Such a solution could be even more profitable to U.S. auto makers than a low mpg, while at the same time doing even more for environmental protection than a high mpg.

**Table 12.5 MPG Standards**

| | GOALS | |
|---|---|---|
| **ALTERNATIVES** | **Conservative**<br>Avoid disruption to profits. | **Liberal**<br>Low pollution. |
| **Conservative**<br>Low MPG standards<br>(20 MPG). | + | − |
| **Liberal**<br>High MPG standards<br>(40 MPG). | − | + |
| **Neutral**<br>Medium MPG standards<br>(30 MPG). | 0 | 0 |
| **SOS or Win-Win**<br>Subsidies to develop high MPG and inexpensive technologies. | ++ | ++ |

# Other Energy Issues

## Providing Heat to the Poor

The problem here is how to provide heat to the poor in the wintertime when poor people cannot afford the heating bills that power companies charge.

The conservative alternative of leaving it up to the marketplace is not likely to provide adequate heat for the poor if this means selling heat below cost. The marketplace, however, may stimulate more efficiency than a socialistic power company that is tax supported, and more efficiency than a regulated utility that is guaranteed a profit in return for accepting regulation.

Socialistic power companies can provide heat below cost as part of their equity obligations, just as the post office delivers mail to rural houses charging less than the actual cost of the mail delivery.

Private ownership with price regulation may lead to inefficiency because the government guarantees a profit in return for artificially low prices. Those prices may be lower than the marketplace, but still not low enough to provide adequate heat for the poor.

**Table 12.6 Heat to the Poor**

| | GOALS | |
| --- | --- | --- |
| **ALTERNATIVES** | **Conservative** Efficient private profit. | **Liberal** Heat for the poor. |
| **Conservative** Marketplace. | + | – |
| **Liberal** Socialistic power companies. | – | + |
| **Neutral** Private ownership with regulation. | 0 | 0 |
| **SOS or Win-Win** Energy vouchers. | ++ | ++ |

A SOS alternative might be to provide poor people with energy vouchers whereby they can supplement what they can afford to pay the power company. Those vouchers consider both the prices of the power company and the ability to pay of the low-income consumer. The voucher system does not interfere with efficient private profit-making companies, but it is capable of providing adequate heat for the poor.

## Locating Undesired Facilities

The problem here is how to get communities to be willing to accept undesired facilities such as a nuclear waste repository, a prison, or a mental health facility. Such facilities may be desirable to have within a society, but people who recognize their need may be unwilling to have such facilities within their communities rather than someone else's community.

The conservative position is generally to resist such facilities because they tend to lower property values. The liberal position may be more receptive to accepting such facilities because they provide job opportunities in the construction and maintenance of the facilities.

Conservatives may be more willing than liberals to accept nuclear reactor facilities in view of conservative support for the nuclear reactor industry. Liberals may be more willing to accept a halfway house for recently released convicts in view of liberal support for rehabilitation. Thus, the nature of the facility partly determines whether it will be resisted or accepted by liberals or conservatives. We should talk about group #1 that resists, and group #2 that accepts, in order to be able to generalize about undesired facilities regardless of their purpose.

The object of a super-optimum solution is to find a way of increasing property values and job opportunities simultaneously while finding locations for facilities that would otherwise be undesired. A reverse auction has those characteristics. A regular auction involves one seller and many potential buyers. The auctioneer starts the price low and moves down until one of the buyers agrees to buy the art object or whatever is being auctioned.

**Table 12.7  Locating Facilities**

| | GOALS | |
|---|---|---|
| **ALTERNATIVES** | **Conservative** <br> Property values. | **Liberal** <br> Job opportunities. |
| **Conservative** <br> Resist. | + | − |
| **Liberal** <br> Accept. | − | + |
| **Neutral** | 0 | 0 |
| **SOS or Win-Win** <br> Reverse auction. | ++ | ++ |

In a reverse auction, there is one buyer and many potential sellers. The buyer starts out with a low offer to pay and moves up until one of the sellers agrees to sell the product to the buyer. This kind of reverse auction is used to get some people who have seats on an overbooked airplane to sell their seats back to the airline so that the plane will no longer be overbooked.

By using a reverse auction, communities can be encouraged to compete for undesired facilities. No community is forced to have the facility. The community that gets the facility is the one that has decided the offering price of the government is high enough to more than offset the drop in property values, or whatever other risks are involved. If the price or subsidy becomes high enough, then the money can be used to lower property taxes, provide for street improvements, and attract additional businesses by using the money for economic development.

The reverse auction can thus increase property values, rather than merely hold them constant, which resisting the facility does. Likewise, the reverse auction can bring in more job opportunities than accepting the facility if the subsidy money is used partly for economic development.

This is a good example of a win-win solution with diverse positions coming out ahead of their best initial expectations. Those expectations include conservative property values, liberal job opportunities, and the interests of the individual and societal beneficiaries of the undesired facilities are conservative or liberal.

# Chapter 13

# Health Care

## Health Care for the Poor and the Middle Class

### Deciding among Alternative Ways of Providing Medical Services to the Poor

Salaried government doctors and no government involvement can possibly be eliminated as not reaching a minimum threshold on political feasibility.

**Table 13.1 (Old) Medical Services to the Poor**

| | GOALS | |
| --- | --- | --- |
| | **Conservative**<br>1. Cost to taxpayer.<br>2. Quality of care. | **Liberal**<br>1. Access<br>2. Cost to consumer. |
| **ALTERNATIVES** | | |
| **Conservative**<br>No government<br>involvement. | + | − |
| **Liberal**<br>Salaried government<br>doctors. | − | + |
| **Neutral**<br>1. Government<br>  reimbursement.<br>2. Government subsidized<br>  insurance. | 0 | 0 |
| **SOS or Win-Win**<br>See text. | ++ | ++ |

Government reimbursement and government subsidized insurance are tied on all the goals because their effects are virtually identical even though the forms are different. Thus gathering additional information about those alternatives or others is not likely to resolve that tie.

This analysis may clarify the need for comparing more specific alternatives such as: (1) the coverage of the reimbursement of insurance, (2) the deductible portion, (3) the control devices to prevent abuses by providers and recipients, and (4) the extent to which group practice is required.

## Evaluating Health Care Policies

Doing nothing means leaving healthcare to the marketplace. Poor people and most middle-class people cannot afford the expensive marketplace charges. Thus doing nothing may lack political feasibility because of voter opposition and the inequities.

**Table 13.2  (New) Health Care Policies**

|  | GOALS | |
| --- | --- | --- |
| **ALTERNATIVES** | **Conservative**<br>Medical profession. | **Liberal**<br>1. Quality of care.<br>2. Access and equity. |
| **Conservative**<br>Do nothing. | + | − |
| **Liberal**<br>Socialized medicine. | − | + |
| **Neutral**<br>Private enterprise with government reimbursement. | 0 | 0 |
| **SOS or Win-Win**<br>1. Government doctors for the poor.<br>2. Medicare supplements. | ++ | ++ |

Socialized medicine means that most doctors are salaried employees of the government providing healthcare in government hospitals. Such a system may lack economic feasibility because it is so expensive, especially with a lack of economic incentives to keep costs down.

Government reimbursement is the system under Medicaid for the poor and Medicare for the aged. It is also highly expensive by handling reimbursement on a case-by-case basis.

The SOS here involves government doctors for the poor. That is a limited form of socialized medicine. It made more sense ten or so years ago. Now one does not have to be poor to be not able to afford medical costs. The SOS suggests expanding Medicare and Medicaid to include more people, possibly through a supplement to what they can afford to pay. That system still has the unnecessary high expense of individual case reimbursement.

As of 1993, a better SOS alternative might be to privatize health care for the poor, the aged, and the middle class, but provide vouchers that can be used to pay for all or part of the insurance in health management organizations or other types of organized clinics. Doing so can provide universal coverage while keeping costs down through competition and insurance per patient rather than per case.

**Health Care Policy: A SOS Perspective**

Table 13.3 refers to health care policy in the context of the Veteran's Administration, but it could apply to health care policy for the poor or middle-class people in general.

Medicare and Medicaid emphasize individuals who go to whatever doctor will service them, and then the government pays all or a high percentage of each case-by-case doctor bill. Such a system tends to be much more expensive than salaried government doctors and is inequitable if it only covers the poor and the aged.

Government-owned hospitals or salaried government doctors tend to be inefficient due to lack of competition. Such a system is also inequitable if it only applies to veterans or poor people since health care expenses can no longer be easily afforded by lower middle-class people or middle-class people in general.

**Table 13.3 (Simple) Health Care Policy**

| | GOALS | |
|---|---|---|
| **ALTERNATIVES** | **Conservative** Privatization. | **Liberal** Equity. |
| **Conservative** Marketplace or Medicare and Medicaid. | + | − |
| **Liberal** Government-owned hospitals. | − | + |
| **Neutral** Both. | 0 | 0 |
| **SOS or Win-Win** Subsidized HMOs. | ++ | ++ |

Subsidized HMOs in this context means the government provides health care vouchers to poor people, aged people, and middle-class people who can qualify. Such vouchers supplement the premiums which HMOs require in order to provide HMO coverage. The HMOs compete with each other, thereby generating lower prices and better quality service. The money for the vouchers can come mainly from employers to cover their own employees, with a provision for covering the self-employed and the non-employed.

**Paying for Expanded Health Care**

The conservative position on paying for expanded health care is no tax increases. The payment should come from eliminating waste. If there is to be a tax increase, it should be on individuals since they will be receiving the health care benefits, and not on corporations.

The liberal position is that a tax increase is acceptable, especially if it is on high incomes. Liberals are also willing to accept taxes on cigarettes and alcohol in order to raise money and discourage smoking and drinking.

**Table 13.4 Paying for Health Care**

| | GOALS | |
| --- | --- | --- |
| **ALTERNATIVES** | **Conservative**<br>Avoid taxes. | **Liberal**<br>Health care reform. |
| **Conservative**<br>No tax increase. | + | − |
| **Liberal**<br>Tax increase OK. | − | + |
| **Neutral**<br>Middling tax increase. | 0 | 0 |
| **SOS or Win-Win**<br>Required premium<br>payments. | ++ | ++ |

The conservative position does well on the conservative goal of avoiding taxes. The liberal position does well on the liberal goal of providing money for health care reform.

To avoid taxes and to provide for expanded health care, one can adopt the SOS alternative of requiring businesses and workers to pay premiums for health care insurance with HMOs or a fee-for-service system. That is like requiring businesses to buy workmen's compensation insurance. It is not a tax that goes to the government; it is a required premium that goes to an insurance company, or to a health care provider who also operates an insurance system.

**Rationing Health Care**

The issue here is what is to be done with someone who is nearly brain dead, but not technically brain dead. If the person were capable of consenting to the withdrawal of life support by way of a living will, then life support would be withdrawn. In this situation, the individual is too young or too unconscious to be able to consent. In some circumstances, it would be appropriate to rely on the consent of parents or other close relatives where there is no conflict of interest.

This issue does not divide traditional conservatives and liberals.

Some conservatives advocate keeping the person alive because withdrawing life support is too much like abortion. Other conservatives are more concerned with the cost to the taxpayer. Some liberals advocate keeping the person alive because a rich person could pay to be kept alive, and poor people should also have that right.

A compromise might be to wait a certain number of days to see what happens, such as thirty days. That does not solve the problem, it just postpones it.

A procedure is needed for arriving at a decision, rather than prolonging a non-decision. Such a procedure might involve a requirement that if three doctors say there is less than 5 in 100 or 1 in 100 odds of the person being able to recover, then life support should be withdrawn.

It is possible that the Clinton health plan will deal with this kind of situation as part of its concern for rationing scarce health care resources. One might also argue that in an affluent society, the cost of keeping such people alive is not such a burden. The benefits of doing so are not only that a solution might develop, but also sending a symbolic message that preserving life and being optimistic are important in a well-functioning society.

**Table 13.5  Rationing Health Care**

| | GOALS | |
| --- | --- | --- |
| **ALTERNATIVES** | **Conservative**<br>Solution can develop. | **Liberal**<br>Save cost. |
| **Conservative**<br>Keep alive. | + | − |
| **Liberal**<br>Pull the plug. | − | + |
| **Neutral**<br>Compromise: 30 days. | 0 | 0 |
| **SOS or Win-Win**<br>3 doctors say less than 1<br>in 100. | ++ | ++ |

# The AIDS Problem

## Evaluating Policies for Dealing with AIDS

Each alternative presented on Table 13.6 has three parts covering testing, discrimination, and prevention. On the subject of testing for AIDS, conservatives have advocated mandatory testing in the workplace and elsewhere. Liberals want only voluntary testing. The SOS involves concentrating on subsidies for vaccines and cures, rather than testing.

On the subject of discrimination against people with AIDS, some conservatives have gone as far as advocating quarantining. Some liberals have gone as far as advocating legislation to prohibit discrim-

**Table 13.6 AIDS**

| | GOALS | |
|---|---|---|
| **ALTERNATIVES** | **Conservative**<br>Decrease AIDS. | **Liberal**<br>Equity. |
| **Conservative**<br>1. Mandatory testing.<br>2. Quarantining.<br>3. Police crackdown. | + | − |
| **Liberal**<br>1. Voluntary testing.<br>2. Anti-discrimination<br>   legislation.<br>3. Privacy. | − | + |
| **Neutral**<br>1. Little testing.<br>2. No legislation.<br>3. Ignore privacy.<br>4. Tolerate arrest. | 0 | 0 |
| **SOS or Win-Win**<br>1. Subsidize for vaccine<br>   and cure.<br>2. Regular anti-<br>   discrimination<br>   legislation.<br>3. Medicalization. | ++ | ++ |

ination against those with AIDS. The SOS might involve relying on
regular anti-discrimination legislation that relates to race, gender, and
disabled people, rather than special legislation.

On the subject of prevention, conservatives tend to advocate
police crackdowns on needle-using drug addicts and places where gay
males congregate like bath houses and gay bars. Liberals are more
negative toward police crackdowns and more tolerant of the privacy
of gays. The SOS might emphasize: (1) treatment and education to
decrease illegal heroin use, (2) safer gay sex to decrease AIDS
transmission among gays, and (3) elimination of traditional venereal
diseases to eliminate the virus transmission belts for transmitting
AIDS from needle users and bisexuals to heterosexuals.


## Alternative Political Campaign Strategies for Dividing between AIDS Dollars and Anti-Discrimination Legislation

The problem here is that gays and those seeking to help them are
divided as to how to appeal for more government-sponsored AIDS
research and more government action against anti-gay discrimination.

**Table 13.7 Campaign Strategies for AIDS**

| | GOALS | |
| | **Conservative**<br>$ for AIDS research. | **Liberal**<br>Reduce discrimination |
| **ALTERNATIVES** | | against gays. |
| --- | --- | --- |
| **Conservative**<br>Gays as a plague. | + | − |
| **Liberal**<br>Gays as good people. | − | + |
| **Neutral**<br>In between. | 0 | 0 |
| **SOS or Win-Win**<br>Gays as a $ threat, but not<br>a disease threat. | ++ | ++ |

One group among the gays advocates communicating AIDS as being an extremely dangerous epidemic that is likely to infect numerous heterosexuals throughout the world if massive action is not taken quickly to find vaccines and cures. That approach may generate research money, but it does not make people more willing to interact on equal terms with gays.

A second group that is more concerned with equalitarian interaction emphasizes that gays are productive people and that AIDS is not likely to be transmitted to heterosexuals. That approach may lessen discrimination against gays but it does not produce the kind of scare that generates a lot of research money.

The SOS alternative should be capable of generating research dollars but also non-discrimination simultaneously. A meaningful way to do that is to emphasize that AIDS among gays and needle users is a monstrous economic threat to the general community because it costs approximately $100,000 to maintain an AIDS patient from the onset of AIDS until they die. That quantity of societal expense should be a big incentive to find a preventive vaccine or cure.

At the same time, it makes sense to communicate to the general public that it is very difficult to transmit AIDS to heterosexuals unless they consort with prostitutes or others who are likely to have traditional venereal diseases that facilitate the passage of the AIDS virus from a female to a male or vice versa.

## A Proposed Super-Optimum Solution to the AIDS Problem

Concentrating on the sexual behavior of homosexuals or the sharing of needles by drug addicts is no longer a meaningful way of large-scale combating of AIDS. The reason being that the saturation point has been virtually reached with regard to how much AIDS the homosexual community and the needle-sharing community already has. It is too late for preventive action for them. The epidemic in those communities has gotten as bad as it possibly can.

Concentrating on a third source of AIDS transmission, namely blood transfusion, is largely meaningless because virtually all blood cleanliness that is possible has been introduced, and virtually no AIDS in the United States of any substantial amount was ever associated with blood transfusions. It occurs in only highly isolated cases that are not transmitted. It creates sensational occurrences, though, because it may involve a six-year-old elementary school child who is barred from attending school thereby becoming a newsworthy event. It was an event of extreme rareness when it was occurring, and now is occurring less, and not likely to result in being transmitted to someone else through sexual behavior or the sharing of needles.

The main current problem with regard to AIDS transmission is the possible beginning of a massive heterosexual epidemic that could be highly devastating. AIDS tends to only get transmitted sexually among heterosexuals if there are already sexually transmitted diseases present that provide a kind of conveyor for the AIDS virus to move from one heterosexual to another or from a bisexual to a heterosexual. Thus, it makes sense to remove the conveyor; this can be done relatively easily with traditional antibiotics, rather than to try to remove the virus. No cure or vaccine has ever been found for any virus, whereas all the traditional sexually transmitted diseases are relatively easy to deal with through antibiotics. Thus, a massive campaign needs to be instituted to eliminate traditional venereal diseases in order to greatly decrease the possibility of the transmission of AIDS.

**Table 13.8  AIDS Problem**

|  | GOALS | |
| --- | --- | --- |
| **ALTERNATIVES** | **Conservative**<br>Save money. | **Liberal**<br>Reduce AIDS. |
| **Conservative**<br>Marketplace. | + | − |
| **Liberal**<br>Big subsidies. | − | + |
| **Neutral**<br>Modern subsidies. | 0 | 0 |
| **SOS or Win-Win**<br>Antibiotics for sexually<br>transmitted diseases. | ++ | ++ |

That is a super-optimum solution by virtue of the fact that it can greatly reduce the increase in AIDS. It does not cure anybody who already has AIDS. At the same time, the cost is very low. A conservative approach emphasizing the marketplace or attempted repression would result in a far higher probability of transmission. It might save money in the short run, but in the long run could greatly reduce societal productivity. A liberal subsidy approach would cost a great deal of money, and (on the basis of past experience) be likely to do very little good. Thus both the conservative and liberal approaches provide very low benefits and very high costs. The proposed SOS approach provides very high benefits at very low costs.

## Requiring HIV Tests for Newborn Infants

The issue here is whether HIV tests should be required for newborn infants. One viewpoint says yes, in order to provide a longer and better life for HIV infants. There is no cure if the HIV virus turns into AIDS. With proper medical care, however, that can be delayed and the child's life can be prolonged and improved.

**Table 13.9 HIV Tests for Newborn Infants**

|  | GOALS | |
| --- | --- | --- |
| **ALTERNATIVES** | **Conservative**<br>Better lives for HIV infants. | **Liberal**<br>Protect privacy of mother. |
| **Conservative**<br>Require tests. | + | − |
| **Liberal**<br>Voluntary tests. | − | + |
| **Neutral**<br>Blind tests. | 0 | 0 |
| **SOS or Win-Win**<br>Voluntary but with persuasion and guardian ad litem. | ++ | ++ |

The opposite viewpoint is the tests should only be voluntary in order to protect the privacy of the mother. If she learns that her infant has AIDS, then she knows she also has AIDS. That can be depressing and even suicidal. Those who advocate only voluntary tests tend to view this conflict as being analogous to the conflict between a fetus and a mother seeking an abortion.

Many states have adopted a neutral position that involves testing newborn infants, but not revealing the information to anyone. That makes information available if the mother requests it. Presumably the blind tests (which do not have infants' names on them) do have identifying numbers so the information can be made available to the mother if requested.

The super-optimum or win-win position whereby both the infant and the mother can come out ahead might involve testing that is not required, but with persuasive incentives to exercise the option. The incentives might include the following:

1. Persuasion that is in the interest of the mother to know whether she has AIDS so she can have her life prolonged and bettered, although not cured.
2. Persuasion that is in the best interest of the child, which the mother should support.
3. Persuasion that is in the best interest of the society for people to know they have AIDS so they can avoid infecting other people.
4. The blind testing facilitates requests for results since one does not have to request the testing.
5. A public guardian can be appointed to represent all newborn children for the purpose of deciding whether the results should be requested in view of the conflict of interest between the infant and the mother. The guardian would have as his major function to persuade (but not coerce) the mother into requesting the results.
6. Persuading the mother to request the results will increase the likelihood of her participating in the medical program to improve the life of the infant.

7. The persuasion might also note that this is not a fetus versus a mother, but rather something closer to the kind of child abuse that occurs when the mother refuses to provide adequate medical care for a preschool child such as a blood transfusion or a vaccination.

# Disease Prevention

## Administering Polio Vaccines in Malawi

Hastings Kazuma Banda is the president for life in Malawi. Partly because he is a former doctor, he believes that only doctors can administer or supervise the administering of polio vaccines. He objects to lawyers or others trying to tell him otherwise.

The more liberal or flexible thinking in Malawi is that polio vaccines can be administered to children by the headman of each village. All he needs to do is to arrange to have the Sabin vaccine poured into cups and given to the children to drink.

**Table 13.10 Polio Vaccines**

| | GOALS | |
|---|---|---|
| | **Conservative**<br>Competence and preserve | **Liberal**<br>Responsive to need. |
| **ALTERNATIVES** | authority. | |
| **Conservative**<br>Doctors. | + | − |
| **Liberal**<br>Headmen. | − | + |
| **Neutral**<br>Nurses. | 0 | 0 |
| **SOS or Win-Win**<br>1. Free speech to suggest<br>     alternatives.<br>2. Headmen with training. | ++ | ++ |

A neutral position would be to use nurses. They, however, are not so available–although more available and less expensive than doctors.

The SOS alternative might be to use the headmen, but provide them with whatever training is needed. That alternative could be responsible to administrative needs and still satisfy the president's concerns.

On a higher level of applicability is the need for more free speech to suggest policy alternatives, without fear of offending a dictatorial president. That kind of free speech could be especially relevant to encouraging more competent handling of policy problems, promoting more respect for the authority of the president, and responding to the need for administrative flexibility.

## Immunization

The basic problem here is that the percentage of young children is not high enough who have received shots immunizing them against various diseases.

The conservative approach emphasizes leaving the matter up to the marketplace. If some families cannot afford adequate immunization, then they should work harder and earn more money so they can afford such health care. The alternative for many conservatives would be to leave the matter to charitable institutions to take care of. Doing so keeps down the burden on the tax payer. It also provides an incentive to pharmaceutical companies to develop better vaccines in order to make bigger profits.

A compromise approach emphasizes having the government administer vaccines through public health personnel and possibly through government manufacturing of the vaccines themselves. Doing so keeps the prices down by eliminating profits. It also facilitates widespread distribution regardless of ability to pay.

Another compromise position would be to have price regulation instead of government employees doing the production and distribution. Price regulation may keep prices down to consumers, but the procedural costs may be an additional expense for the pharmaceutical

**Table 13.11  Immunization**

|  | GOALS | |
|---|---|---|
| **ALTERNATIVES** | **Conservative**<br>1. Decrease tax costs.<br>2. Increase business incentives. | **Liberal**<br>1. Reduce prices down.<br>2. Increase distribution. |
| **Conservative**<br>Marketplace. | + | − |
| **Liberal**<br>1. Government manufacturing.<br>2. Public health personnel. | − | + |
| **Neutral**<br>Price regulation. | 0 | 0 |
| **SOS or Win-Win**<br>Contracting out the manufacturing and distribution. | ++ | ++ |

companies and the taxpayers. Price regulation can also decrease business incentives.

The super-optimum solution (where both sides can come out ahead of their best initial expectations simultaneously) may involve contracting out both the manufacturing and the distribution of the vaccines. The government would give the production contract to the lowest bidder who can meet the quality specifications. That would tend to keep consumer prices down as well as government costs, while simultaneously providing a competitive incentive to do well in order to obtain the profitable manufacturing contract. Likewise, the distribution contract goes to the lowest bidder who can meet the quality specifications. Doing so can result in widespread distribution at lower prices and tax costs than if the government sought to do the distributing itself.

## Allocating National Dollars across Provinces to Decrease Infant Mortality

The population figures are as of 1980. Each number represents millions of people.

The reputational efficiency figures are measured on a 0-10 attitudinal scale. They are hypothetical figures that could be obtained by asking knowledgeable insiders who are associated with reducing infant mortality across the states.

The allocation figures in the last column are expressed in thousands. Thus the total budget is $10 million, of which Alabama gets $117,000.

Population is not a goal to be increased. It is a criterion for equitably allocating funds independent of how efficiently the money is used.

**Table 13.12    Allocating National Dollars across Provinces to Decrease Infant Mortality**

| Criteria | Population | | Efficiency | | Sum of P/W %s | Allo-cation %s (Sum/2) | Allo-cation |
|---|---|---|---|---|---|---|---|
| Alternatives | Raw Score | Part/ Whole Percent | Raw Score | Part/ Whole Percent | | | |
| 1. Alabama | 3.7 | 1.65% | 2 | .69% | 2.34% | 1.17% | $117 |
| 2. Alaska | .4 | .18 | 5 | 1.72 | 1.90 | .95 | 95 |
| 3. Arizona | 2.4 | 1.07 | 7 | 2.41 | 3.48 | 1.74 | 174 |
| . | | | | | | | |
| . | | | | | | | |
| . | | | | | | | |
| 49. Wisconsin | 4.7 | 2.10 | 8 | 2.76 | 4.86 | 2.43 | 243 |
| 50. Wyoming | .5 | .22 | 7 | 2.41 | 2.63 | 1.32 | 132 |
| Totals | 223.9 | 100.0% | 290 | 100.0% | 200.0% | 100.0% | $13,000 |

Note: The details are not given for all the states because we are just trying to illustrate the allocation method. That can be done with just the five states shown here.

## Deciding an Optimum Level of Cancer in Light of the Prevention and Damage Costs

As cancer cases increase, lost productivity goes up at a constant rate and patient medical care goes up at a diminishing rate. In order to get cancer down, prevention cost has to go up at an increasing rate.

Considering these three relevant costs and the above data, the optimum cancer level is 300 cases per whatever population is under consideration. At that level, the total costs are minimized at fifty-eight monetary units.

An important point is that the optimum level of cancer is zero cases only if the cost of achieving zero cases is low, which it is not. The zero category would be the optimum category if the prevention costs at that point were fifty-seven, which would be contrary to having a higher prevention cost with 100 cancer cases.

**Table 13.13    Deciding an Optimum Level of Cancer in Light of the Prevention and Damage Costs**

| Goals<br>Alternatives(X) | Lost<br>Productivity<br>$Y_1 = .1(X)$ | Patient<br>Medical Care<br>$Y_2 = (X)^{.5}$ | Prevention<br>Cost<br>$Y = 1\mu(X)^{-2}$ | Sum |
|---|---|---|---|---|
| $    0 | $    0 | $    0 | $  -- | $  -- |
| 100 | 10 | 10 | 100 | 120 |
| 200 | 20 | 14 | 25 | 59 |
| 300 | 30 | 17 | 11 | 58 |
| 400 | 40 | 20 | 6 | 66 |
| 500 | 50 | 22 | 4 | 76 |

# Special Issues

## A SOS of Animal Experimentation in Health Care Policy

Both conservatives and liberals as of 1993 condemn the torture of animals, including practices like bear-baiting or cock-fighting. Thus they tend to support organizations like the Anti-Cruelty Society or the Humane Society.

The issue here, however, is the use of animals to test new medicines or medical procedures. Conservatives tend to endorse experimentation, although some conservatives may feel more sympathy toward abused animals than humans who are poor or discriminated against. Liberals tend to advocate prohibitions or restrictions on animal experimentation, although the issue of animal experimentation does not divide conservatives and liberals as clearly as issues that relate to economic policy.

The weights here are not the conventional weights for conservatives and liberals. They are only a half unit apart, rather than two units. Both conservatives and liberals are on the pro side of the goal of human well-being, although conservatives more so. Both are on the relatively con side of animal well-being in comparison to human

**Table 13.14  Animal Experimentation**

|  | GOALS | |
| --- | --- | --- |
| **ALTERNATIVES** | **Conservative**<br>Human well-being. | **Liberal**<br>Animal well-being. |
| **Conservative**<br>No animal rights. | + | – |
| **Liberal**<br>Prohibit animal<br>experimentation. | – | + |
| **Neutral**<br>Guidelines. | 0 | 0 |
| **SOS or Win-Win**<br>1. Develop simulation.<br>2. Human volunteers. | ++ | ++ |

well-being, although liberals more so.

The object of an SOS alternative in this context is to have a policy that will promote human well-being by having medicines and medical procedures effectively tested, while at the same time minimizing the need for animal experimentation. Some of that can be done through more use of simulation. For example, one can determine the effects of the drugs and X-rays on cancer cells by observing what happens to cancer cells in a test tube or a petri dish, without having to inject cancer cells into a mammal. If there is no effect in that simulation, one can probably reject the drug. If there is an effect then one might try it on human volunteers who already have cancer. Likewise, numerous other examples can be given where meaningful experiments can be conducted using some kind of controlled simulation or human volunteers, more than may be currently done.

## Public Policy toward Suicide

Group #1 consists of: (1) conservatives who may endorse prohibiting suicide for religious reasons and (2) liberals who may have secular reasons such as the possibility of recovery and avoiding bad examples.

Group #2 consists of: (1) conservatives who advocate non-interference by government in victimless crimes and (2) liberals who consider the right to commit suicide by consenting adults as a civil liberty related to the right to privacy.

A neutral position would allow for individuals to reject extraordinary means to keep them alive, especially if they are incurably and painfully ill.

The SOS solution involves reducing the need for prohibiting or allowing suicide by reducing the causes of suicide. That means more effective public policy toward dealing with such matters as unemployment, poverty, homelessness, health care, and family disputes.

Table 13.15 and the accompanying analysis could also apply to the typical right-to-die case. The issue is whether to pull the plug on someone whose life is being sustained by extraordinary equipment such as a respirator or dialysis machine. The SOS of removing the

**Table 13.15  Suicide**

| | GOALS | |
| ALTERNATIVES | Conservative<br>Possibility of recovery. | Liberal<br>Civil liberties right. |
| --- | --- | --- |
| **Conservative**<br>Prohibit. | + | − |
| **Liberal**<br>Allow. | − | + |
| **Neutral**<br>Living will. | 0 | 0 |
| **SOS or Win-Win**<br>Lessen the causes of<br>suicide. | ++ | ++ |

causes of suicide is not so applicable to that situation, assuming that the ability to breath or perform other essential bodily functions cannot be restored. An optimistic position would say never pull the plug unless there is a zero possibility of recovery. A pessimistic position might allow pulling the plug in the absence of a living will where three relevant doctors declare there is less than a five percent chance of recovery. A neutral position might say less than one percent. A statute could specify the needed degree of probability, but preferably very low. A low probability encourages the saving of lives as being a more important value than hospital costs or somebody's inconvenience.


## Organ Transplant Banks

Table 13.16 was generated by an article in *The American Enterprise* for December 1993. It endorses establishing a marketplace for organs in order to relieve the organ transplant shortage.

Conservatives advocate money incentives in this context. Liberals advocate incentives based on altruism without monetary rewards. The compromise would be some money, but not as much as the market might bring.

The main conservative goal is to make more organs available to those who can buy them. The main liberal goal is to prevent exploitation of people who are desperate for money. This could include people who jeopardize their health by giving organs while they are alive, or who accelerate their death in order to obtain money for their families.

A SOS is needed that could generate a lot more organs, but provide no monetary rewards that lead to exploitation. Perhaps a big difference could be made if there were widespread publicity as to how healthy people at any age could sign a form to donate their organs after they die. There may be many people who would be willing to do so, but they do not know how to do so.

Along with that SOS, there could be included a health-care system that enables both poor people and rich people to have equal access to organs by way of HMOs or other insurance plans. Such a system avoids discrimination against either poor recipients or poor donors.

**Table 13.16  Organ Transplants**

| | GOALS | |
|---|---|---|
| **ALTERNATIVES** | **Conservative**<br>More organs. | **Liberal**<br>No exploitation. |
| **Conservative**<br>Money. | + | – |
| **Liberal**<br>Altruism. | – | + |
| **Neutral**<br>Some money. | 0 | 0 |
| **SOS or Win-Win**<br>Publicize. | ++ | ++ |

## Allocating a National Budget between Training Doctors versus Nurses

Constraints:

1. The total budget is considered to be $2 million.
2. The cost of training one doctor is considered to be $100,000, and the cost of training one nurse is considered to be $10,000.
3. For one doctor to function efficiently, it is considered necessary to have five nurses, which is roughly the same as seventy nurses to thirteen doctors rounded to the nearest whole doctor.

Perspectives:

1. If life expectancy were the only criterion, then 75 percent of the budget would go to training doctors and 25 percent to nurses. By giving life expectancy a weight of four, the allocation is 70 percent and 30 percent, which is only five percentage points away from the maximum. The weight of four can thus be considered as the convergence value of the weight of life expectancy since it is the smallest weight that is within .05 of the allocation limits.
2. The optimum allocation if constraint #3 did not exist would be to allocate 75 percent of the budget to doctors and 25 percent of the budget to nurses without considering the training cost per doctor and per nurse. Those training cost figures are only relevant to how many doctors one receives for 75 percent of a $2 million budget, and how many nurses one receives for 25 percent. This is a problem in which the costs are fixed by constraints #1 and #2. The object is to allocate so as to maximize benefits (i.e., life expectancy) given those costs. Regardless whether column four is 59 percent and 41 percent or 75 percent and 25

**Table 13.17    Allocating a National Budget between Training Doctors versus Nurses**

| Goals Policies | Life Expectancy (W=2) | | Training Cost (W=2) | | Sum of Weighted P/W%s | Allo-cation | Quantity | Adjusted for Con-straints |
|---|---|---|---|---|---|---|---|---|
| | Relative Score | P/W % | Relative Score | P/W % | | | | |
| Doctors | 3 | 75% | 10 | 91% | 59% | $1.18 | 12 | 13 |
| Nurses | 1 | 25% | 1 | 9% | 41% | $0.82 | 80 | 70 |
| Totals | 4 | 100% | 11 | 100% | 100% | $2.00 | | |

percent, the final allocation is thirteen doctors and seventy nurses in order to satisfy constraint #3.

3. One does not allocate the whole $2 million to doctors. Doing so would be contrary to the principle of diminishing returns, whereby additional dollars tend to produce a lower marginal rate of return. One can prove that if the part/whole percentages are treated as proxies to the elasticity coefficients, then one should allocate in proportion to those P/W percents.

# Chapter 14

## Technological Innovation

### Alternative Approaches to Learning Reality

#### A SOS Analysis of the Epicureans versus the Stoics

Table 14.1 analyzes the historical and philosophical controversy that goes back to the ancient Greeks as to what is the ideal lifestyle. The Epicureans emphasize non-work pleasure, whereas the stoics emphasize work.

The compromise position is to divide one's waking hours between the two orientations. Thus, one might spend about eight hours per day in pleasure activities like eating and entertainment. One might spend another eight hours in work, and the third eight hours in sleep.

A SOS position might be to develop a technological fix which will enable one to increase both the pleasure hours and the work hours by reducing the sleep hours. This may involve some genetic engineering that changes the need for sleep to be no more than approximately two hours a day. That will leave eleven hours for constructive work and eleven hours for pleasure activities, or at least more than eight for each.

This is a good example of a super-optimum solution through expanding the resources available, with time being the scarce resource in this situation. One can then do more of each of the activities or budget categories that were formerly fighting over a smaller pie or budget. This particular technology is not currently available, but progress has been made in recent years in developing

**Table 14.1 Epicureans versus Stoics**

| ALTERNATIVES | GOALS | |
| --- | --- | --- |
| | **Conservative** Be productive, active, and self realization | **Liberal** Satisfy need for food and sleep. |
| **Conservative** Apollonian or Stoic (productive activity). | + | − |
| **Liberal** Dionysian or Epicurean (sleep, eat, and entertainment). | − | + |
| **Neutral** Compromise. | 0 | 0 |
| **SOS or Win-Win** Health, but no sleep and fast food. | ++ | ++ |

a better understanding of sleep, which seems to occur more because it is genetically programmed than because it serves a useful function.

Another SOS solution might be to arrange for as many people in society as possible to be doing work that they consider highly pleasurable. The ideal arrangement might be for everyone to have the kind of job that they would continue to do even if they were independently wealthy and did not need the money. That might require public policy that upgrades the quality of skills and the quality of workplaces. This is an example of a SOS that may not be attainable for everyone or even a society as a whole, but it is worth striving for.

## Choosing among Research Approaches

A verbal approach in policy evaluation may involve: (1) a historical description of what policies have been adopted, (2) a legal analysis of what policies might be constitutional or in conformity with prior statutes or precedents, or (3) a philosophical approach that emphasizes the good and bad aspects of various policies.

**Table 14.2 Research Approaches**

| ALTERNATIVES | GOALS | |
| --- | --- | --- |
| | **Conservative**<br>Broad, practical impact. | **Liberal**<br>Causal understanding. |
| **Conservative**<br>Verbal descriptive research. | + | − |
| **Liberal**<br>Quantitative descriptive research. | − | + |
| **Neutral**<br>Verbal and quantitative descriptive research. | 0 | 0 |
| **SOS or Win-Win**<br>Policy science research. | ++ | ++ |

A quantitative approach in policy evaluation may involve: (1) a statistical analysis of the relations among variables relevant to a given policy, (2) a mathematical model that deduces conclusions from certain axioms that are generally intuitively accepted, or (3) an analysis associated with operations research or management science that involves relating quantitative variables to a single objective function or goal.

The policy science approach referred to above includes: (1) working with multiple criteria or goals rather than a single objective function, (2) using simple qualitative scoring so that important goals can be considered on which more quantitative data is not available, (3) seeking to arrive at solutions whereby all major sides of a policy problem can come out ahead of their best initial expectations simultaneously, (4) using multiple alternatives, what-if analysis, decision-aiding software, and decision matrix analysis, and (5) showing a concern for getting policies adopted and successfully implemented.

**Rationalism, Incrementalism, and SOS Analysis**

Rationalism in public policy evaluation tends to emphasize developing a comprehensive list of goals to be achieved, alternatives available for achieving them, and relations between goals and alternatives in order to choose the best alternative.

Incrementalism tends to emphasize trying an alternative to determine its effects. If those effects are satisfactory, then the alternative is adopted. If those effects are not satisfactory, then another alternative is adopted.

SOS analysis involves: (1) having a couple of alternatives as a starter, generally including a conservative and a liberal alternative, (2) having a couple of goals as a starter, generally including a conservative and a liberal goal, and (3) relating the goals to the alternatives in a rough way, (4) in order to arrive at tentative conclusions, and (5) subject to being improved through what-if analysis.

The what-if analysis may involve: (1) adding, subtracting, combining, or dividing goals, (2) doing likewise with the alternatives, and (3) changing the scoring system or the specific scores on the relation scores or the relative weights of the goals.

**Table 14.3  Rationalism and Incrementalism**

|  | **GOALS** | |
| --- | --- | --- |
| **ALTERNATIVES** | **Conservative**<br>1. Formality<br>2. Foresightful | **Liberal**<br>Flexibility. |
| **Conservative**<br>Rationalism. | + | − |
| **Liberal**<br>Incrementalism. | − | + |
| **Neutral**<br>Half and half. | 0 | 0 |
| **SOS or Win-Win**<br>100% of both. | ++ | ++ |

## Deduction versus Induction

Deduction involves drawing conclusions from premises that are empirically verified or intuitively accepted.

Induction involves drawing conclusions by generalizing from many specific examples.

A combination approach may involve sometimes using deduction and sometimes using induction depending on which best fits the situation.

The SOS involves always using both deduction and induction in drawing all conclusions. In the context of policy evaluation, this could mean deduction in processing goals, alternatives, and relations to arrive at a best alternative. It also means that the goals, alternatives, and especially the relations are based on generalizing from many specific examples.

## Classical Philosophy versus Quantitative Analysis

The notes on "Deduction versus Induction" provide a more detailed analysis.

**Table 14.4 Deduction and Induction**

| | GOALS | |
|---|---|---|
| ALTERNATIVES | Conservative<br>Internal consistency. | Liberal<br>External validity. |
| Conservative<br>Deduction. | + | − |
| Liberal<br>Induction. | − | + |
| Neutral<br>Combination. | 0 | 0 |
| SOS or Win-Win<br>100% of both to all<br>problems. | ++ | ++ |

## Table 14.5  Classical Philosophy and Quantitative Analysis

| | GOALS | |
|---|---|---|
| **ALTERNATIVES** | **Conservative**<br>Causal understanding. | **Liberal**<br>Pragmatic usefulness. |
| **Conservative**<br>Classical philosophy<br>(deduction). | + | − |
| **Liberal**<br>Quantitative analysis<br>(inductive). | − | + |
| **Neutral**<br>Descriptive behavioral<br>process. | 0 | 0 |
| **SOS or Win-Win**<br>SOS analysis. | ++ | ++ |

## Generalizations versus Case Studies in Developing Knowledge

Generalizations versus case studies is a controversial issue in the developing of new knowledge, but those two concepts do not lend themselves to conservative and liberal labels. Liberals tend to emphasize induction since it is normally associated with empirical observation. Conservatives tend to emphasize deduction since it is normally associated with reasoning from authoritative axioms.

The two key purposes of developing new knowledge are for better causal understanding and for broad practical knowledge. Those goals are also difficult to associate with the labels of conservative or liberal. Business conservatives emphasize practical knowledge. Intellectual liberals emphasize causal understanding. Within the same scholarly discipline, however, conservatives may advocate knowledge for knowledge sake. The liberals may then advocate knowledge that has implications for public policy or practical affairs.

Whether the alternatives and goals are labeled conservative, liberal, position #1, or position #2, the SOS alternative might be a cyclical approach. Case studies lead to generalizations, but then generalizations are applied to specific situations that add to the

**Table 14.6  Generalizations versus Case Studies**

| | GOALS | |
|---|---|---|
| **ALTERNATIVES** | **Conservative**<br>Causal understanding. | **Liberal**<br>Broad practical<br>knowledge. |
| **Conservative**<br>Generalizations. | + | − |
| **Liberal**<br>Case studies. | − | + |
| **Neutral**<br>Middle range. | 0 | 0 |
| **SOS or Win-Win**<br>Cyclical approach. | ++ | ++ |

case studies including the exceptions to the generalizations. Those new case studies reinforce or modify the generalizations, which then get applied to new case situations, and so on. The result is likely to be better causal understanding than just relying on generalizations, and simultaneously better practical knowledge than just relying on case studies.

# Stimulating Creativity

## The Patent System and Encouraging Inventions

Preserving the patent system (as it is currently operating) tends to stifle some creativity by providing for a seventeen-year monopoly renewable once, but frequently renewed repeatedly with slight variations. It also stifles creativity by being the basis for lawsuits designed to obtain injunctions against creative competition. Abolishing patents can hurt some creativity on the part of people who develop new inventions in order to obtain a monopolistic patent, although as of 1990 those new inventions may be for relatively small matters rather than for new forms of transportation, communication, energy, or health care.

**Table 14.7 Patent System**

| | GOALS | |
|---|---|---|
| **ALTERNATIVES** | **Conservative** Decrease taxes. | **Liberal** Creativity. |
| **Conservative** Preserve patents. | + | − |
| **Liberal** Abolish patents. | − | + |
| **Neutral** Change systems. | 0 | 0 |
| **SOS or Win-Win** Well placed subsidies to encourage technology. | ++ | ++ |

Well-placed subsidies could mean calling a conference of leading scientists and engineers to develop a list of 50-100 important needed inventions. The government could then announce the availability of grants and other monetary rewards to encourage the development of those inventions. The rewards could be worth more than a monopolistic patent while encouraging (rather than stifling) competition.

Changing the system by shortening the patent monopoly, requiring licensing, or having the government as an insurer against product liability can be helpful, but not as much as well-placed subsidies to encourage needed inventions.

## Alternatives for Product Liability

Common law defenses enable manufacturers to escape liability by arguing: (1) they did not sell directly to the consumer, (2) contributory negligence by the consumer, (3) third party partially responsible, and (4) implicit waiver of the right to sue.

Strict liability means the manufacturer is liable for damages to the consumer if the product injured the consumer, regardless of the above common law defenses.

## Table 14.8  Product Liability

| | GOALS | |
| ALTERNATIVES | **Conservative**<br>Stimulate innovation of product. | **Liberal**<br>Safety and compensation. |
|---|---|---|
| **Conservative**<br>Common law defenses. | + | – |
| **Liberal**<br>Strict liability. | – | + |
| **Neutral**<br>Common law defenses with exceptions or comparative negligence. | 0 | 0 |
| **SOS or Win-Win**<br>Strict liability after 3 years of marketing. | ++ | ++ |

Comparative negligence means the consumer collects even if the consumer is partly negligent, as long as the part if less than 50 percent

The SOS alternative mentioned here provides for strict liability only after three years of marketing in order to stimulate product innovation and provide a time period for debugging product defects. A better SOS alternative might be to have the government be an insurer for the first three years so as to provide better compensation to injured persons while freeing product innovators from liability if they exercise reasonable care.

## Handwork versus Assembly Lines in Developing Nations

The conservative Gandhi position is to emphasize hand-crafted work. Doing so may not be high in productivity, but it provides quality workplaces in terms of safety, dignity, and being free of pollution.

The liberalized position is to emphasize assembly-line work associated with industrialized societies. Doing so may be high in productivity, but often lacks safety, dignity, and cleanliness.

**Table 14.9  Handwork versus Assembly Lines**

| ALTERNATIVES | GOALS | |
| --- | --- | --- |
| | Conservative<br>Productivity. | Liberal<br>Quality workplace. |
| **Conservative**<br>Hand-crafted work. | + | − |
| **Liberal**<br>Assembly line work. | − | + |
| **Neutral**<br>Cottage industries with<br>small machines. | 0 | 0 |
| **SOS or Win-Win**<br>Highly automated<br>assembly plant. | ++ | ++ |

The compromise is working at home but with machines that work off electric outlets. Such machines are more productive than hand looms while at the same time not so unsafe, undignified, or unclean as factories.

The SOS alternative might be to have highly automated assembly plants like Japan. Such plants do even better on productivity than traditional assembly lines, and generally better on safety, dignity, and cleanliness than electric machines. Also see Table 7.7.

# Desirable Research

## Stimulating Socially Useful Research

The SOS emphasizes socializing people at an early age to want to discover new and useful knowledge. That means an emphasis on creativity and usefulness in elementary and secondary education.

Doing so is likely to result in more socially useful research than either pure market forces or making subsidies available, although such socialization can be combined with the stimulus of a free market and the facilitating value of a well-placed subsidy.

**Table 14.10    Socially Useful Research**

| ALTERNATIVES | GOALS | |
|---|---|---|
| | **Conservative**<br>1. Freedom.<br>2. Save taxes. | **Liberal**<br>Usefulness. |
| **Conservative**<br>Laissez-faire encouraging<br>what is easy. | + | − |
| **Liberal**<br>1. Big funding for causal.<br>2. Policy research. | − | + |
| **Neutral**<br>Both. | **0** | **0** |
| **SOS or Win-Win**<br>1. Socialization with free<br>market.<br>2. Subsidies. | ++ | ++ |

## Validity versus Ethics in Experimental Social Science

The concrete example here is trying to experimentally determine the effects of being incarcerated (versus being granted probation) on the probability of repeating one's crime.

Paid incarceration (rather than randomly forced incarceration) is needed to meet the ethical problems, but doing so can interfere with the meaningfulness of the experiment.

To offset the bias that has been introduced by paying those who consent to incarceration over probation, one needs to statistically adjust for differences in the demographic and attitudinal characteristics between the two groups.

One also has to observe lagged recidivism, since repetition of one's crime may be delayed as a result of funds available to those incarcerated.

**Table 14.11  Validity versus Ethics**

|  | GOALS | |
| --- | --- | --- |
| **ALTERNATIVES** | **Conservative** Validity. | **Liberal** Ethics. |
| **Conservative** Random. | + | − |
| **Liberal** Do not conduct. | − | + |
| **Neutral** Compromise. | 0 | 0 |
| **SOS or Win-Win** Paid incarceration. | ++ | ++ |

## Validity and Simplicity in Policy Analysis

Validity in policy analysis refers to internal consistency in drawing a prescriptive conclusion from goals, alternatives, and relations. It also refers to external consistency between the alleged goals, alternatives, and relations on the one hand and empirical reality on the other.

Simplicity in policy analysis refers to having as few goals, alternatives, and relations as are needed to capture the essence of the policy problem. Simplicity also includes an emphasis on simple arithmetic rather than calculus, operations research, or statistical analysis if possible.

Frequently policy analysts think of increasing validity by decreasing simplicity, or increasing simplicity by decreasing validity. The approach of using a decision matrix or an SOS table may provide greater validity by including goals that are normally difficult to work with using complex methods. Such goals may, however, be relatively easy to work with if simple methods are used that allow for a substantial margin of error.

**Table 14.12  Validity and Simplicity**

|  | GOALS | |
| :--- | :--- | :--- |
| **ALTERNATIVES** | **Conservative** <br> Form. | **Liberal** <br> Democratic <br> understanding. |
| **Conservative** <br> Validity. | + | – |
| **Liberal** <br> Simplicity. | – | + |
| **Neutral** <br> Half and half. | **0** | **0** |
| **SOS or Win-Win** <br> Striving for 100% on <br> both. | ++ | ++ |

## Criteria for Evaluating Policy Analysis Research

See the previous related tables for some relevant notes. All the tables in this section relate to standards for judging the quality of research in general and policy analysis research in particular.

The standards include usefulness, validity, ethics, simplicity, importance, and whether the research is adopted. The closest table is Table 14.12 on validity versus simplicity as alternative standards. This is in contrast to the present table, Table 14.13, which compares validity with importance, adoption, and utilization.

The previous table has as its goals proper form versus causal understanding, whereas the present table has as its goals proper form versus social impact. Both tables endorse the idea of striving for all those goals simultaneously, rather than sacrificing some of a goal to achieve more of another goal.

Validity was defined in the previous table, as well as simplicity. Importance refers to whether the research deals with big societal benefits in terms of either social impact or causal understanding. Adoption refers to whether the recommendations of the research are adopted, regardless whether the research is referred to. Utilization refers to the research being actually cited, regardless whether it is

**Table 14.13  Evaluating Policy Analysis**

|  | GOALS | |
| --- | --- | --- |
| **ALTERNATIVES** | **Conservative** Proper form. | **Liberal** Social impact. |
| **Conservative** Validity. | + | − |
| **Liberal** 1. Importance. 2. Adoption. 3. Utilization. | − | + |
| **Neutral** Compromise. | 0 | 0 |
| **SOS or Win-Win** Striving for 100% on both. | ++ | ++ |

adopted. The ideal research should be valid, simple, important, adopted, and acknowledged.

   Those characteristics are desirable because they lead to research that has social impact, causal understanding, and proper form.

# Special Issues Relevant to Technology Innovation

### Deciding on a Space Policy for NASA

   Conservatives tend to advocate expanding U.S. space policy mainly because they view the program as being relevant to U.S. national stature in the sense that Sputnik was relevant to USSR stature and the moonwalk was relevant to past U.S. stature. Liberals, on the other hand, tend to advocate decreasing the program since they view it as too closely related to wasteful defense expenditures, when there is a need for more spending on domestic policy problems. The neutral position is to hold constant the space expenditures, rather than increase or decrease them.

   A SOS alternative might be to expand the space program, but direct it more toward developing marketable products. This could

**Table 14.14  Space Policy**

| ALTERNATIVES | GOALS | |
|---|---|---|
| | **Conservative**<br>National stature. | **Liberal**<br>Spend for domestic programs. |
| **Conservative**<br>Expand. | + | − |
| **Liberal**<br>Contract. | − | + |
| **Neutral**<br>Hold constant. | 0 | 0 |
| **SOS or Win-Win**<br>Expand toward marketable projects. | ++ | ++ |

include space stations for manufacturing metals and pharmaceuticals under conditions that are more favorable than manufacturing such products on earth. Improved conditions include a totally clean atmosphere and weightlessness with less gravity and friction.

Emphasizing products made under those circumstances can improve U.S. stature by being a leader in that kind of manufacturing. If the quantity of products expands, the addition to the national income could be substantial. That has the possibility for providing additional funds for domestic problems and also for providing additional tax revenue by way of the expanded tax base.

Other commercially valuable projects might include mining activities on the moon or the nearest planets. That would require more investment of money and time, but the payroll may be worth it. Other commercial uses of space relate to improved communications and the possibility of a microwave platform in the sky with laser beams to send solar energy across the earth. The solar energy platform could be a big income producer.

These commercial projects can be contrasted with less commercially valuable projects that relate to ballistic missiles, star wars, searching for extraterrestrial life, astronomy applications, or putting

**Table 14.15  Stability and Modernization**

| | GOALS | |
| | **Conservative**<br>1. Minimize disruption.<br>2. Labor relations.<br>3. Families.<br>4. Crimes.<br>5. Congestion.<br>6. Environment. | **Liberal**<br>1. Benefits of<br>    modernization.<br>2. Health.<br>3. Education.<br>4. Crime. |
| **ALTERNATIVES** | | |
| **Conservative**<br>Stability (stagnation). | + | − |
| **Liberal**<br>Modernize fast<br>(disruption). | − | + |
| **Neutral**<br>Modernize slow. | 0 | 0 |
| **SOS or Win-Win**<br>1. Well-placed subsidies.<br>2. Tax breaks<br>    emphasizing quality. | ++ | ++ |

a man on the planets. Those may be worthwhile projects but they are not as relevant to the goals of the above SOS table as expanding the space program in the direction of commercially worthwhile products.

## Stability and Modernization in Developing Nations

Well-placed subsidies and tax breaks in this context especially refer to: (1) upgrading the skills of workers mainly through on-the-job training, including workers who are displaced by new technologies, and (2) facilitating the adoption of new technologies that create jobs, improve productivity, or increase exports.

Emphasizing quality refers to: (1) workplace safety and quality, (2) environmental quality, and (3) quality products.

# Index

# About the Author

Stuart S. Nagel is professor emeritus of political science at the University of Illinois at Urbana-Champaign. He is secretary-treasurer and publications coordinator of the Policy Studies Organization and coordinator of the Dirksen-Stevenson Institute and the MKM Research Center. He holds a Ph.D. in political science and a J.D. in law, both from Northwestern University. His major awards include fellowships and grants from the Ford Foundation, Rockefeller Foundation, National Science Foundation, National Social Science Council, East-West Center, and the Center for Advanced Study in the Behavioral Sciences. His previous positions include being an attorney to the U.S. Senate Judiciary Committee, the National Labor Relations Board, and the Legal Services Corporation. He has been a professor at the University of Arizona and Penn State University.